TOOLKIT FOR TACKLING RACISM IN SCHOOLS

Stella Dadzie

Trentham Books

First published in 2000 by Trentham Books Limited
Reprinted 2001, 2002, 2004, 2005

Trentham Books Limited
Westview House
734 London Road
Oakhill
Stoke on Trent
Staffordshire
England ST4 5NP

British Cataloguing in Publication Data
A catalogue record for this book is available from
the British Library
ISBN 1 85856 188 4

Designed and typeset by Trentham Print Design
Ltd., Chester and printed in Great Britain by
Bemrose Shafron (Printers) Ltd., Chester.

ACKNOWLEDGEMENTS

I could name a number of women and men whose love of learning or commitment to fighting racism have inspired me in my work. Although unnamed, they are not un-remembered. May this book do justice to their vision of all that our schools and our society could be.

I am particularly indebted to Gillian Klein for her consistent support, enthusiasm and encouragement; and to the following individuals who were willing to take time out of their busy schedules to read and comment on the text. Their feedback was invaluable – and most gratefully received.

Paul Boyd, former teacher, currently Director of Quality Educational Consultants, Barnet

Henderson Clarke, Ethnic Minority Achievement Teacher, Cardinal Wiseman RC High School, Middlesex

Caroline Dargan, Education Consultant, formerly Head Teacher of North Harringey Junior School, London

Valerie Davies, Principal Inspector, London Borough of Ealing Education Services

George Martin, African-Caribbean Leadership Council and Governor of Fortismere School, Haringey

Berenice Miles, Senior Projects Officer, London Borough of Ealing Education Services

Robin Richardson, Consultant, Commission on the Future of Multi-Ethnic Britain

Andrew Robinson, former teacher in Lambeth and the Caribbean

Stella Dadzie
November 1999

CONTENTS

PREFACE

This *Toolkit* is the outcome of over twenty years' work in schools, colleges, youth clubs and other educational settings. It is also a response to several requests I've received since the publication of *Racetracks*[1] to produce a similar resource for teachers – something practical and accessible that not only suggests why we should be tackling racism in schools but also gives some practical, user-friendly guidance as to how.

Racism is a complex social reality with a long and painful history and it would be arrogant to suggest that there are any 'off-the-peg' answers. Yet for lack of access to practical guidance, teachers can spend much time 'reinventing the wheel'. Thanks largely to the efforts of those teachers, parents and activists who have fought for change, often against the most difficult of odds, there is now a recognised body of good practice for schools to draw from. Moreover, schools have been grappling with issues of 'race', racism, culture and identity for many years, so there is also an established pedagogy. Even a cursory overview of its history suggests that the case for antiracism has been firmly established. The challenge to schools in the 21st century is to translate it into a viable day-to-day practice.

The past four decades have been characterised by the search for meaningful policies and procedures that will guide schools and other institutions in their efforts to outlaw discrimination. As the emphasis in the curriculum shifts increasingly towards the development of the whole child, with a global awareness and active citizenship skills, perhaps it is time to move on. Schools are uniquely placed to both shape and define tomorrow's citizens – but harmonious, tolerant, peaceful human relations will only come about when people are afforded their basic human rights and guaranteed justice and equal treatment. As we move towards our vision of a more just and equitable multicultural society in this new millennium, there is a need to take stock of our progress – and to reassess the vital role teachers can play in helping to eliminate the racism that has so blighted children's lives throughout the 20th Century. This antiracist toolkit will, I hope, be a small contribution to that process.

x

INTRODUCTION

1 AIMS and OBJECTIVES

AIMS

The aims of this *Toolkit* are to provide teachers in secondary schools with a flexible and accessible resource that

- ❑ can be used in a variety of teaching and/or staff development contexts, both formal and informal

- ❑ encourages teachers and students to question their own and others' views about racism

- ❑ suggests some practical, positive ways of tackling racism as a whole-school issue

- ❑ provides a set of desired outcomes against which schools can assess their strengths and weaknesses and 'measure' their performance

OBJECTIVES

PART ONE of the *Toolkit* is aimed primarily at teachers and their managers or advisors. It sets out to

- ❑ raise awareness of the legal and educational case for antiracism

- ❑ suggest some practical strategies for tackling institutional racism and promoting equality and positive relations in your school

- ❑ encourage you to consider the context, resources and development work necessary for this to be effective

- ❑ identify some appropriate outcomes for planning, target-setting or self-assessment purposes

PART TWO suggests some approaches and learning activities that teachers can use to address racism and related topics in a classroom setting. If you follow the advice on planning and preparation, the units and individual exercises will help you in your efforts to encourage students to

- ❑ explore the historical roots of racism and how racist ideas and stereotypes have evolved

- ❑ understand the need to challenge racism in school as well as at home and on the streets

- ❑ appreciate the benefits of having a positive sense of cultural identity

- ❑ accept personal responsibility for their own attitudes and behaviour towards others

2 TARGET GROUP

This resource is most suitable for secondary school teachers and others who support their work with young people aged 11-16 years. It should be of particular relevance to staff involved in policy development, planning and review, staff development and similar activities, including

- ❏ classroom teachers
- ❏ headteachers and other education managers
- ❏ staff responsible for curriculum development
- ❏ teachers and pastoral staff
- ❏ teacher trainers
- ❏ PSE/ Curriculum Advisors

Although developed with teachers in mind, there are many others who influence young people's personal development who may find the suggested approaches and activities of interest – for example

- ❏ staff development co-ordinators
- ❏ people involved in teacher and youth worker training
- ❏ parents and carers
- ❏ youth and community education workers
- ❏ residential social workers
- ❏ college lecturers and tutors

3 HOW TO MAKE BEST USE OF THIS *TOOLKIT*

The *Toolkit* consists of two self-contained sections. The Units in Part 1 are primarily for use in staff or institutional development contexts, while the Units in Part 2 suggest different activities that can be used when exploring racism in the classroom.

You can use them in a variety of contexts to help structure or stimulate departmental, team-based, focus group, tutor group and PSE discussions. They should encourage everyone in your school – governors, managers, staff and students – to think about racism and how they handle it.

As you explore each section, you will find that they each consist of a combination of

- ❏ introductory notes
- ❏ good practice checklists
- ❏ staff training activities
- ❏ practical classroom exercises or assignments
- ❏ suggested resources, including ideas for further reading and some useful contacts

Desired outcomes are summarised at the start of each section and highlighted throughout the text in bold. They can be used in a variety of ways – for example, when preparing for inspection, reviewing progress or for planning and self-assessment purposes.

To make best use of this *Toolkit*, use it for...

ORGANISATIONAL DEVELOPMENT

PART ONE of *Toolkit* focuses on whole-school responses. It will be of most use in **strategic planning forums, governing body meetings, INSET or working party discussions.** The different activities and checklists are sign-posted and can be used to review your school's Equal Opportunities/Antiracist policy and explore school-wide practices and procedures*. The accompanying notes highlight some practical responses and present a 'nutshell' case for their adoption. Ideally, you should aim to work through each Unit systematically, using the checklists as a stimulus for strategic change and organisational development. If this is not possible, groups and individuals will still benefit from selecting the Units or activities most relevant to their school, and using them to initiate a formal or informal debate about how to achieve the outcomes listed at the beginning of each Unit. Working through each Unit should help you to identify practical measures that will be appropriate to your school, its context and its community. Where these measures are already in place, use the checklists to help you to evaluate and review your progress and identify new priorities.

STAFF DEVELOPMENT

Many of the tasks and checklists in Part One will also be useful for **INSET, staff development and staff induction** purposes. They should help raise awareness of the case for policies, procedures and practices. They will also help to stimulate ideas about how to deliver these in a competent way. The checklists suggest a structure for these discussions which are best conducted in small groups. Sadly, the opportunities for formal staff development of this kind are sorely limited in some schools, particularly where managerial support for this work is lukewarm. It is hoped that individuals working in isolation or without the backing of their Head Teacher will still find the notes and checklists helpful when considering their personal practice or preparing to argue the case in meetings or other forums.

PERSONAL DEVELOPMENT

Many of the tasks in Part One and some of the activities in Part Two can be used for **self-assessment, self-directed learning** or **personal development** purposes. If you are unfamiliar with the issues or feel you lack the confidence to articulate them, you could opt to work through the different Units alone or in **dialogues with a manager, mentor, colleague or appraiser.** This will help to raise your awareness of racism and how it operates, but if you are new to this field and want to expand your knowledge base, you will also benefit from doing some of the suggested reading.

CURRICULUM DEVELOPMENT

PART TWO consists of five self-standing yet complementary units that can be used to raise students' awareness of different aspects and experiences of racism. The SUMMARY at the beginning of each Unit will assist staff involved in **curriculum development activities** by suggesting the awareness and attitudinal changes that should underpin any introductory course of this kind. You may want to supplement these with ideas and messages of your own. Alternatively, use them to help you determine the most appropriate units or activities for different year groups to work through, either as **part of a tutorial programme or a PSE course** or to augment the curriculum in **other subject areas.**

---

*   The Checklists in this *Toolkit* may be photocopied and reproduced for staff training purposes.

LESSON PLANNING

Each unit consists of

■ SUMMARY

Use this information to help you to pinpoint the awareness and attitudinal changes
you are aiming for and to determine the most appropriate units or activities for your
group. It will also help you when introducing the different units or clarifying
objectives and teaching outcomes

■ TEACHING OUTCOMES

Use these for lesson and curriculum planning purposes, and when evaluating
individual units or activities. They will also help you to identify the most appropriate
activities and to distinguish between essential and desirable outcomes.

■ PROMPTS

Use these to explore specific topics, as a basis for structuring discussions and when
preparing the group for follow-up work.

■ DISCUSSION TOPICS

Use these to raise awareness of the issue and encourage critical thinking. They will
also give you ideas when preparing materials and back-up resources, identifying topics
for assignments or project work and thinking about follow-up activities, further
research, project work, homework or class assignments

■ CLASSROOM ACTIVITIES

Use these activities (or develop your own) to consolidate what has been learnt. The
methods and approaches outlined will give you ideas for project, course, homework
and assignments and when planning lessons and future courses.

■ CHECKLIST: THINGS TO DO

Use these checklists to help you prepare and to identify any resources you will need
on the day. You may also want to refer to the supplementary list of BOOKS and
RESOURCES at the end of the *Toolkit*, since they will help you identify other sources,
alternative activities and ways of tackling themes in greater depth. The list is not
exhaustive, but it is a starting point for anyone wishing to expand their knowledge in
this area.

4 CONTEXT

'...all schools should be informed by a policy that recognises the pernicious and all-pervasive nature of racism ...and the need to confront it'
Macdonald Inquiry 1989

'It is incumbent on every institution to examine their policies and practices to guard against disadvantaging any section of our communities ...there must be an unequivocal acceptance of the problem of institutional racism and its nature before it can be addressed...' Macpherson Report, 1999

■ Antiracism: a brief overview[2]

Concerns about how to tackle racial discrimination in education have been dogging education providers ever since 1962 when '**Boyle's Law**'[3] gave credence to the notion that the presence of black students in British schools lowered standards. By the time **Bernard Coard** drew attention to the discriminatory treatment of West Indian students in the late 1960s[4], educationalists already perceived the 'problem' to be one of either linguistic or cultural deficiency, ignoring the possibility that racism might be a contributing factor. Since then, **black parents** have campaigned long and hard for measures to counter the effects of discriminatory attitudes and low expectations in schools. Where their concerns and suggestions fell on deaf ears, they worked alongside black teachers to set up **Supplementary** or **Saturday Schools** or organised **Black Studies, Home Language** or **Religious Instruction courses** within their own communities. Some parents entrusted their children to private or church schools in the belief that these would offer them a better chance in life. Later, when responses to racism became more institutionalised, a few chose to become parent governors in the hope of influencing school and LEA policies.

Inside schools, the efforts of a small but vocal group of teachers to promote **multicultural education** slowly began to raise awareness of eurocentrism in textbooks, paving the way for new developments in the curriculum. Their efforts were often aided by teachers employed under **Section 11** funding[5] which provided financial support to schools with a substantial number of New Commonwealth or 'immigrant' students. Although Section 11 staff were primarily employed to respond to language needs, they brought with them a new awareness that permeated many other areas of the curriculum.

Slowly, other teachers began to take note of non-Christian festivals and to find ways of exploring the contributions of people from 'Third World' cultures in the classroom. In some schools a '**steel bands and samosas**' approach[6] became the substitute for addressing the more thorny issue of institutional racism. Showing children how to put on saris or listening to Bob Marley in assembly has invariably proven easier than tackling problems like racial harassment in the playground or the disproportionately high school exclusion rates for African-Caribbean boys.

By 1981 – albeit somewhat tentatively – the **Rampton/Swann Committee**[7] was publicly acknowledging institutional racism – defined as 'practices (that) may be adopted by public bodies as well as be private individuals which are unwittingly discriminatory against black people' – as a contributing cause of black underachievement. Many Local Education Authorities (LEAs) responded by appointing **Multicultural Advisors** (also known also as Multi-ethnic or Minority Ethnic advisors) and **Multicultural Curriculum Support Units**. Others established special Advisory Units whose function was often limited, due to their lack of executive powers, to the development of paper policies and the circulation of unenforceable advice. In some schools, **Race Awareness Training** – often poorly conceived or ineptly delivered – came to be seen as a universal panacea, spawning a defensiveness that would resurface ten years later in a staff-room backlash against 'political correctness'.

Throughout the 1980s, a number of high-profile debates and inquiries helped to keep issues of 'race' in the public eye. The **1989 Macdonald Inquiry** into the playground murder of schoolboy Ahmed Iqbal Ullah at Burnage High School had a particularly lasting legacy. Critical of the school's 'moralistic and doctrinaire' approach to **anti-racism**, the Macdonald report called for more sensitive, sophisticated practices that took account of other factors such as class, gender, age and size. This critique was seized upon by the media as evidence that antiracism 'doesn't work'. *The Daily Telegraph* went as far as to claim that the school's antiracist policies had *'led to a killing'*, while other national newspapers slated Labour-led authorities for promoting an obsessive and divisive creed. Unfortunately, this view prevailed, despite the best efforts of the Macdonald team to reassert its conclusion that *'all schools should be informed by a policy that recognises the pernicious and all-pervasive nature of racism ...and the need to confront it'*.

Multiculturalism, while seen as a softer, more palatable response, has also come in for public criticism. In 1992, when a white parent objected to her child being taught Asian language songs at a **Cleveland** primary school, the High Court dismissed a CRE complaint against the local LEA's decision to support her. Although the issue was Cleveland's refusal to acknowledge that the motives for this parent's objections were racist[8], the High Court's critique of the school centred instead on questions of language and culture. In doing so, it not only distracted public attention away from concerns about institutional racism within the LEA, but effectively condemned multiculturalism for detracting from, rather than enriching, the education of white children.

There has also been much controversy over the collection of ethnic data on students. The DES has had schools first collecting, then abandoning, then reinstating **ethnic monitoring**, leaving education researchers and policy-makers with large gaps in the data they rely on to assess performance and determine national policy. There remain serious inconsistencies both in relation to the ethnic categories used and the focus of such monitoring. The unacceptably high **school exclusion figures** for black adolescent boys of African-Caribbean origin are a case in point. Voiced as an anecdotal concern by teachers, parents and education pressure groups for many years, the statistical data that would confirm the extent of the problem and strengthen the case for schools and LEAs to find strategic responses, have only recently begun to be collected by the DfEE on a national basis.[9]

Macpherson's report following the **Stephen Lawrence Inquiry** has again revived the debate about how this might be done. Stephen Lawrence's murder by a group of white peers has been seen by antiracists as a damning indictment of the education system. In 1991, four years before he was stabbed to death at a bus-stop in Eltham, Home Office figures revealed a marked increase in the number of racial assaults, threats, vandalism and other forms of racial abuse. 30% of these were perpetrated by children or juveniles under the age of 15[10]. Only three years before, in 1988, a major national report had found **racial harassment** to be pervasive within the education system, and 'a blight on the lives' of students, parents and staff.[11] Clearly, despite the best efforts of those who have tried to find ways of addressing the issue over the past thirty years, the question of how schools are to tackle institutional racism remains as high a priority as it ever was.

While the fundamental issues haven't changed much since the Rampton/Swann report, both the context and the political climate for antiracist work in schools have. Since the **1988 Education Reform Act** introduced sweeping educational reforms, even LEAs with the political will no longer have the powers to impose **Equal Opportunities policies and**

procedures on their schools. This has led to a patchy and inconsistent response across the country and a gap between policy and practice that has been condemned by HMI as 'unacceptably wide'.

Today, the priorities continue to shift as Headteachers parry the effects of inadequate budgets, damaging OFSTED reports and poor performance in the school league tables. Teachers, particularly in inner city State-funded schools, frequently complain of 'burn-out', brought on by the administrative demands of the National Curriculum, staff shortages, inadequate resources and the pressure to produce academic results at the expense of other less 'marketable' success criteria. Faced with insufficient time, staff-room inertia and genuine confusion about how best to confront the issues, even the most committed of teachers have had to reconsider their priorities. For some, antiracism has dropped way down the list. For others, it has become subsumed within the more palatable rhetoric of **social exclusion**, diversity management, 'education for world citizenship' or generic Equal Opportunities debates.

Thirty years on, black parents, governors, teachers and advisors continue to express concerns about underachievement, unjust school exclusions and the failure of many schools to respond to their childrens' cultural, religious and linguistic needs. They have also been among the most vocal critics of the **National Curriculum**, fearing that its centrally-imposed definitions and assessment systems could reverse many of the hard-won gains of the 1980s. Addressing the implications of Macpherson's recommendation that the National Curriculum should better reflect the needs of our diverse, multi-ethnic society represents one of the key challenges for the millennium to teachers in schools.

Beyond the school gates, the media-driven campaign against '**political correctness**' has revived public distrust of antiracism, undermining initiatives to promote anti-discriminatory policies and practices in schools. The period during the 1980s when ILEA and other Labour-run LEAs actively promoted antiracist and other Equal Opportunities initiatives is typically portrayed as an era of municipal lunacy.[13] Conscious of this 'loony left' legacy and of their increasingly competitive context, schools have generally become less assertive in their efforts to address racism. If Macpherson's call for schools to make the goal of challenging racism and valuing diversity central to their practice is to be heeded, significant changes in the 'mindset' of many teachers will be needed, as well as the time and resources to develop new ways of working.[14]

Thankfully, many teachers have been wrestling with these issues since the early seventies, and although some have had to fight solitary battles, there have been some resounding success stories. A cursory overview of the antiracist campaigns and controversies that have characterised the past thirty years may present a discouraging picture, but the prospects for the new millennium are by no means bleak. Antiracism may be patchy, under-resourced and frequently under attack, but there is nevertheless a wealth of **good practice** around the country for schools to draw from.

Because of these efforts, no area of **the school curriculum** has escaped scrutiny, to the extent that today even the most recalcitrant of colleagues would find it hard to argue convincingly that their subject is 'neutral'. Defying their more cynical judges, classroom teachers have found ways of transforming the attitudes of their students and the ethos of their schools. There have been similar successes in the playground and the boardroom. When cuts in spending and staffing have threatened these endeavours, schools have been aided by **explicit policies, supportive Headteachers, approving parents, enthusiastic students** and **clear-sighted governors**. Thanks to their vision and tenacity, we are now able to see concrete evidence of what can be achieved when schools set out to challenge racism in a way that touches and empowers their students' lives.

This *Toolkit* sets out to both consolidate and complement these endeavours. It does not claim to present all the answers and there are undoubtedly many gaps and oversights. But if used with care and forethought, it should help support efforts to develop and consolidate a more consistent antiracist practice. Equally important, as we enter the 21st century and move towards a more tempered and holistic view of humanity, it should give young people, whatever their ethnic background, the confidence to tackle racism in their schools and combat it in their lives.

References

1 *RACETRACKS: A Resource for Tackling Racism with Young People* by Stella Dadzie (LB Greenwich, 1993) was written for Youth Workers and has been widely used within the Youth Service

2 This overview is inevitably a superficial account of a complex and multi-faceted subject. Readers who want to know more are strongly urged to make use of the suggested reading list to explore the events and initiatives referred to in greater depth.

3 In 1963, Edward Boyle, then Minister of Education, declared in Parliament that it was 'desirable' on educational grounds that no school should have more than 30% of immigrants. Responding to complaints by white parents in Southall about the large number of Asian children in a particular school, the Minister's efforts to 'prevent this happening elsewhere' gave credibility to the idea that black students were a problem and that their presence in schools prevented the progress of their white peers.

4 Coard's board, '*How West Indian Children are made Educationally Sub-Normal in the British Educational System*' (New Beacon Books, 1971) exposed the widespread practice of referring West Indian (nowadays referred to as 'African-Caribbean') children, often on arrival, into 'ESN' schools or units on the assumption that if a child spoke Patois, they lacked the intellectual capacity to cope with the mainstream curriculum.

5 Under Section 11 of the 1966 Local Government Act, local authorities could apply for special funding to support the employment of additional staff necessary to respond to 'the presence within their areas of substantial numbers of people from the Commonwealth whose language or customs differ from those of the rest of the community'. The funding has undergone a number of changes, culminating in huge cuts that have resulted in the loss of Section 11 staff and the termination of numerous projects.

6 'Steel bands and somosas' was the term originally used to attack the multicultural approaches adopted by a small number of primary schools in the late 1970s.

7 The initial terms of reference of the Rampton/Swann Committee was to give 'attention to the educational needs and attainments of students of West Indian origin'. The interim report, *West Indian Children in Our Schools* (sic) was given a cool reception by the DES and was heavily criticised by teachers and black educationalists for its naïve understanding of racism and its negligible impact on education policy.

8 In correspondence to Cleveland LEA, the parent concerned wrote: 'I don't think it's fair for her to go through school with about four white friends and the rest Pakinstan(sic)....I don't think it's right when she comes home singing in Pakistan (i) ...I want her to go to a school where there will be the majority white children, not Pakistan(i)...'

9 DfEE figures suggest that African-Caribbean students are currently three times more likely to be excluded from school (6.6 per 1000) than their white counterparts (1.8 per 1000).

10 *British Crime Survey*, HMSO, 1991

11 *Learning in Terror*, CRE, 1988

12 A typical example is the ridicule some schools have faced when attempting to promote non-discriminatory language or introduce curriculum resources that reflect social diversity.

13 The Ethnic Minority and Travellers Achievement Grant, administered by the DfEE via local education authorities, which replaces the Home Office's Section 11 funding, provides an ideal opportunity for schools to bid for these resources

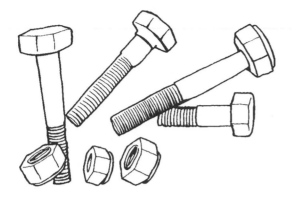

PART ONE

NUTS AND BOLTS

'the essential or practical details'
(Collins Concise Dictionary)

WHAT'S IN PART ONE?

This half of the *Toolkit* addresses the essential and practical aspects of developing a school-wide response to racism. It sets out

- ❏ to raise awareness of the legal and educational case for antiracism
- ❏ to suggest some practical strategies for tackling institutional racism and promoting equality and positive relations in your school
- ❏ to encourage you to consider the context, resources and development work necessary for this work to be effective
- ❏ to identify some **desireable outcomes** for planning, target-setting, review or self-assessment purposes

The tasks and checklists (see next page) will be of particular use if you are involved in

- ❏ developing or revising school policies
- ❏ reviewing progress in the identified areas
- ❏ identifying new priorities
- ❏ establishing school-wide Equality targets or goals
- ❏ planning for strategic change or development
- ❏ facilitating staff or curriculum development activities
- ❏ evaluating existing practices and procedures
- ❏ identifying and consolidating good practice
- ❏ seeking practical responses to specific concerns
- ❏ seeking the views of members of the School Council

Use the OUTCOMES listed at the start of each Unit to identify the tasks and activities that are likely to be most relevant to your school's needs and current stage of development.

SIGNPOSTS:

 ORGANISATIONAL DEVELOPMENT   PERSONAL DEVELOPMENT

 STAFF DEVELOPMENT   CURRICULUM DEVELOPMENT

1

WHAT'S IN PART ONE?

UNIT 1: Meeting Legal Requirements

■ 1.1.What does the law say?

Antiracism is not simply a moral or humanitarian issue. There is a strong legal case for taking a firm stance against racism which, in the current climate of litigation and undisclosed payouts, schools would be unwise to ignore. When **the Head Teacher, School Governors and managers understand the legal and statutory arguments for tackling racism and take a lead in this area**, it is more likely that staff and students will take the issue seriously.

Racial discrimination is outlawed under **Article 14 of the European Convention for the Protection of Human Rights and Fundamental Rights and Freedoms** to which all European member states, including the UK, are signatories.

It is also unlawful under **The Race Relations Act** (1976) which makes both direct and indirect discrimination on grounds of race, colour or nationality (including citizenship) or ethnic or national origins illegal.

The Education Reform Act (1988) requires school governing bodies to discharge their responsibilities without racial discrimination and to ensure that no unlawful discrimination takes place in their school.

■ 1.2 Who is included?

Exactly who is included in the legal definition has had to be established through case law. The House of Lords has defined the term 'ethnic group' as people who have ...

❑ a long shared history

❑ a cultural tradition of their own

Other relevant characteristics include:

- a common geographical origin, or descent from a small number of common ancestors
- a common language
- a common religion

For the purposes of the Act, this definition also includes Travellers.

■ 1.3 Who must comply?

All educational establishments, including schools, colleges and universities, are covered by the RRA. **Section 17 of the Race Relations Act** requires that education providers do not discriminate

- in the terms on which they offer admission
- in refusing to accept an application
- in the way students or students are afforded access to any benefits, facilities or services
- by excluding them from the establishment or subjecting them to any other detriment

It is important that **managers understand the need to use carefully targeted monitoring to scrutinise the school's performance** in each of these areas (see Unit 4, Monitoring)

■ 1.4 What is 'unlawful discrimination'?

The law identifies two forms of unlawful discrimination:

Direct Discrimination involves treating people less favourably than others on the grounds of their 'race', colour, nationality (including citizenship) or because of their ethnic or national origins. It takes many forms, and may vary from crude racist comments to subtle differences in how students are assessed or treated. This may be unconscious or well-intended, but it is still unlawful. Sections 30 and 31 of the Act also make it unlawful to instruct or put pressure on others to discriminate.[1]

Indirect discrimination involves applying a rule, condition or requirement which, although applied equally to everyone, has an adverse or discriminatory effect on a particular racial group, making it difficult for them to comply. This could involve enforcing a certain dress code or a school timetable that does not take account of a pupil's religious obligations, for example.[2] The Race Relations Act makes indirect discrimination on the grounds of 'race' illegal unless there is an 'objective justification' – i.e. unless it can be justified on educational or other objective grounds.

■ 1.5 What are the implications for school governors?

As employers, school governors are liable for any discriminatory act by an employee in the course of his or her employment in the school. The fact that a discriminatory act was done without their knowledge or consent provides no defence in law, unless they can show that **the school has considered all reasonably practicable steps to prevent discrimination** from occurring. Such steps would include, for example, staff development and regular briefings about Equal Opportunities, racial harassment procedures, and the systematic monitoring by ethnic group of pupil intake and achievement.

To prevent accidents and avoid dangers that could disable a pupil or damage their health, managers must abide by important Health and Safety laws. These require

schools and other institutions to take the safety and welfare of staff and students seriously and to display essential information such as who to contact in the event of an accident in all public areas. As Stephen Lawrence's murder graphically demonstrated, for both the perpetrators and their victims, racism is no less damaging or disabling. Your school's response to racism, whether from staff or students, should therefore be just as uncontentious – and just as rigorous. When managers are able to convey the need for staff to actively respond to racism with the same rigour as a Health and Safety issue, you will know your school is making significant progress.

■ 1.6 CHECKLIST: COULD WE BE BREAKING THE LAW?

The CRE's Code of practice for the Elimination of Racial Discrimination in Education gives several examples of racial discrimination in schools, as defined in law, some of which have been reproduced in the checklist below. Use it to establish whether you are applying any practices, procedures or requirements in your school that could be unwittingly unlawful. **Bear in mind that, in most cases, the examples given here would be considered unlawful only if there were no objective justification (e.g. Educational, academic, health and safety grounds).** If your ticks or queries suggest this is not the case, your LEA-school link officer or a CRE advisor can help you establish whether there is a need to take remedial action to ensure that your school is acting fully within the law.

Do we	✔
Apply any **entry criteria, conditions or requirements**, whether academic or non-academic, that might exclude ethnic minority students or reduce their chances of admission?	
Require parents who are foreign nationals to produce **passports or other documentary evidence** as proof of their children's entitlement to the education we provide?	
Only accept students from a **catchment area** that does not include any ethnic minority communities?	
Enforce a **uniform code** that might adversely affect students who are unable to comply for religious reasons?	
Insist on certain **types of clothing** for PE and similar activities that could exclude certain children from taking part?	
Remove **students for whom English is an additional language** from mainstream provision for reasons that cannot be justified on educational grounds?	
Apply **diagnostic and academic assessment criteria** that are culturally biased or result in the non-admission or over-referral of students from a particular racial group?	
Apply **disciplinary criteria** that result in the suspension or exclusion of a disproportionately high number of students from a particular racial group?	
Apply **criteria for allocating individuals to sets or streams** that result in a disproportionately high number of students from a particular racial group being placed in lower streams or sets or channelled into particular subject areas?	
Allow **employers** providing work experience placements, who reject or discourage referral of students from a particular racial group, to go unchallenged?	
Know of any other practices or procedures in the school that could be unwittingly discriminatory?	

■ 1.7 What happens if staff or parents complain?

Your school should have well-publicised complaints procedures for parents and grievance procedures for staff wishing to complain about unfair treatment. To be able to make a complaint without fear of victimisation is an entitlement, and people are more likely to make use of them if your school's **complaints and grievance procedures are transparent, efficient and fair** in all respects. It is vital that **managers understand the importance of logging and analysing complaints about racial discrimination from parents, students or employees,** so that discriminatory trends or patterns can be detected. This ensures that the overall success of your policy in reducing such occurrences can be periodically monitored. It also provides crucial evidence in the event of a formal investigation.

The CRE (Commission for Racial Equality) has the power to investigate allegations of direct and indirect racial discrimination and publish their findings. They can also assist individuals who wish to bring complaints of racial discrimination before a county court (or sheriff court in Scotland). Complaints about treatment at work are heard in Employment Tribunals. The cost of discrimination is not just financial. CRE investigations and tribunals involving allegations of racial discrimination, however unfounded, can be a huge embarrassment if publicised. Whether proven or unfounded, it may take years for a school to rid itself of the negative reputation it acquires.

■ 1.8 What happens if students complain?

Ideally, there will be similar procedures for students who wish to complain about racial harassment, bullying, verbal or physical threats and other forms of intimidation. However, the fear of being labelled a 'grass' may be greater than the desire for justice, so students will need to be encouraged and empowered to use such procedures. One way of overcoming this is to require that **staff respond fairly and consistently to all racial incidents,** however trivial they may seem, **and keep a detailed record of all racially-motivated incidents,** whether reported or witnessed. Young people are less likely to resort to such behaviours in an environment that actively discourages antisocial behaviour. There should be no automatic assumption that colleagues will know how to avoid or resolve conflicts and it is important that **staff receive clear, consistent guidance and regular staff development** so that pro-active (rather than reactive) strategies can be explored and boundaries agreed. This is important not only to reduce inter-racial conflict among students but also to discourage confrontational behaviour by white staff who do not always respond appropriately themselves when tackling inappropriate behaviour.

Above all, a clear message needs to go out that **the school takes racism and other forms of unacceptable behaviour seriously**. This means having procedures and mechanisms in place to record, respond to and monitor such incidents, and involving all the players – students, parents and staff – in the school's efforts to reduce them.

1   In July 1987, the CRE successfully brought proceedings against British Electrical Repairs (BER) in the Westminster County Court on the grounds of applying pressure on a school to discriminate. This case involved school students seeking work experience placements as part of the Certificate of Pre-Vocational Education (CPVE). When Selhurst High School contacted the manager of BER, he agreed to placements for two students at the factory to gain work experience and invited the teacher responsible to visit the factory to finalise arrangements. When it emerged that the two boys were of African-Caribbean origin, the manager said that the workforce would not accept them and that it would not be a good idea to proceed. The incident was referred by the LEA to the CRE. When the case came to court, a declaration was granted that a contravention of the Act had occurred, under section 331 and the defendants were ordered to pay costs. It should be noted that it would be unlawful for a school to yield to such pressure, whatever the motive. The CRE's legal powers are set out in their publication *Enforcing the Race Relations Act*.

2   In Mandla –v- Dowell Lree (1983) the House of Lords ruled that a refusal by a school to admit a Sikh boy because he insisted on wearing a turban constituted indirect racial discrimination under section 17 of the RRA because it disregarded the custom and practice of his racial group. The requirement could not be justified on objective grounds. Although religious discrimination is not unlawful per se, this case illustrates how religion may be relevant in identifying discrimination on racial grounds and may therefore be challenged under the RRA.

■ 1.9 CHECKLIST: DO WE TAKE RACISM SERIOUSLY ENOUGH?

Use the following checklist to establish whether your schools' procedures for preventing, recording and responding to racial harassment and other unacceptable behaviour by students are up to the task. You may want to add your own criteria.

Do we...	✔
Have a well-publicised **Code of Conduct** linked to a Behaviour Policy that specifies what constitutes racial harassment and other unacceptable behaviours and outlines the sanctions that will apply if these are ignored?	
Encourage **pupil involvement** in regular discussions about the school's behaviour code and what should be in it?	
Have an **Incidents Book** in which staff are actively encouraged to record the details of any racially-motivated incident?	
Keep a record of the **ethnic groups of those involved**, and note any **action(s) taken?**	
Have procedures in place for **offering immediate support to the target or victim** and **informing their parents or carers?**	
Have sanctions and procedures in place for discouraging, counselling and/or **re-educating perpetrators** and **informing their parents or carers?**	
Include details of the school's grievance or complaints procedures in **staff induction and INSET** to ensure that all staff are aware of their responsibilities for implementing them?	
Encourage staff to discuss **ways of tackling harassment**, verbal abuse, bullying, intimidation, fighting and other unacceptable behaviours in a firm yet non-confrontational way?	
Encourage students to consider their personal experiences of these behaviours and to identify **appropriate ways of responding** as part of their PSE, education for citizenship or tutorial curriculum?	
Include details of the school's grievance or complaints procedures in **information to parents** and involve them actively in agreeing the underlying principles that inform them?	
Encourage staff and students to play an active role in creating a school ethos and environment that is safe and 'inclusive'	
Other suggestions?	

■ 1.10 How does this fit in with Statutory Requirements?

Despite concerns about the status of antiracism in schools following the Education Reform Acts of 1986 and 1988 and the introduction of National Curriculum, the statutory case for giving this work priority status has been convincingly made. There is copious guidance from the DfEE on how schools are expected to interpret statutory requirements. There are also Government funds available from your LEA, which can be accessed by making an bid for a share of the Ethnic Minority and Travellers Achievement Grant.

The inevitable gap between the intentions behind the legislation and its practical implementation will only be closed if teachers and their managers can access available resources, and receive the guidance and support they need from their LEAs to respond to the challenge. The statutory guidance may, at times, appear ambiguous but the references to culture, identity, diversity, multiculturalism, equal opportunities and, most recently, world citizenship and inclusivity, present a clear message of intent:

Overview of statutory requirements

The curriculum of a school satisfies the requirements of the (Education Reform) Act if it is a balanced and broadly based curriculum which:

a   **Promotes the spiritual, moral, cultural, mental and physical development of students at the school an of society; and**

b   **Prepares such students for the opportunities, responsibilities and experiences of adult life**

Education Reform Act, 1988

A commitment to providing equal opportunities for all students and a recognition that preparation for life in a multicultural society is relevant to all students should permeate every aspect of the curriculum

National Curriculum Council, 1990

(Multicultural education) ...seeks to prepare all students for life in a world where they will meet, live and work with people of different cultures, religions, languages and ethnic origins

National Curriculum Council, 1991

The establishment of harmonious race relations in the most effective schools ...(requires) ...a wide range of purposeful and constructive strategies. Included within these strategies are...

- **positive behaviour management policies**
- **regular and appropriate in-service training**
- **a multicultural and antiracist curriculum**
- **close parental and community links**
- **pupil organisation which takes account of ethnic and gender balance**
- **the boosting of students' self-esteem; books and materials which avoid stereotypical and inaccurate images**
- **school social events aimed at pulling together the difference life experiences of groups within the community**
- **staffing establishments which reflect, as far as possible, the ethnic make-up of the school and the community**

Raising the Attainment of Minority Ethnic Pupils, OFSTED, 1999

UNIT 2: Developing Your Policy

OUTCOMES

Completing this Unit will help you to develop an Equal Opportunities (Antiracist) policy that

✔ serves as a public declaration that the school takes racism and other forms of discrimination seriously

✔ provides an explicit framework for whole-school change and development

✔ is used as a consultation, planning and self-assessment tool and as a formal yardstick against which to assess progress

✔ addresses discrimination in all its forms

✔ actively informs the day-to-day life and work of the school

✔ is seen as realistic and achievable by staff, parents and students

✔ was developed and is actively supported by those who are expected to implement it

✔ is easy to understand and appropriate for different audiences and uses

Policy-making is not, of itself, a panacea but where staff are seriously involved in the development and implementation of policies they clearly benefit from the process ...their own awareness of racial issues is often raised along with commitment to dealing with them. Raising the Attainment of Minority Ethnic Students, OFSTED Report, 1999

9

■ 2.1 Why have a policy?

Many a working party has laboured hard to produce carefully worded Equal Opportunities, Antiracist or Multicultural policies that have little significant impact on their school. So why have a policy? It is easy to subscribe to a declared commitment to outlawing racial inequality and other forms of discrimination. Translating these good intentions into a viable and visible everyday practice, however, relies on more than written declarations.

Despite this persuasive (and much-heard) argument, your school's published commitment to combating racial and other forms of discrimination should be seen as an important first step. **Your Equal Opportunities/Antiracist (EO/AR) policy serves as a public declaration** to parents and guardians, external contractors, examination bodies, prospective and actual staff, the local community and, most important of all, to the young people who walk through the gates each morning **that the school takes racism and other forms of discrimination seriously.**

■ 2.2 What should a policy be used for?

Declaring your school's intentions is only a starting point, but if your policy is comprehensive in its scope and actively informs planning, monitoring and self-assessment activities, it can provide **an explicit framework for whole-school change and development:**

✔ **CONSULTATATION**
Used as **a consultative tool**, for example, it can help staff and students to articulate their concerns and suggest aspects of school life they want to change.

✔ **MONITORING**
Used as **a basis for monitoring achievements**, exclusions, staffing and other key areas, your policy can provide a framework for the systematic scrutiny of your school's performance against its declared intentions

✔ **INSPECTION and SELF-ASSESSMENT**
In inspection, auditing or **self-assessment** exercises, establishing how well your policy is implemented is often a starting point for identifying strengths and weaknesses; the vibrancy and effectiveness of your policy also serves as a evidence.

✔ **PLANNING**
As a **planning tool**, it provides a blueprint for change by suggesting a structure and rationale for establishing targets, procedures and relevant initiatives.

✔ **REVIEW**
If it is regularly reviewed, it will also serve as **a formal yardstick against which to assess your progress** and update your school's strategic priorities.

■ 2.3 What should our policy say?

Although most likely to be part of your school's Equal Opportunities policy, your school's declared commitment to challenging racial discrimination and promoting positive 'race' relations should be in the form of an explicit, self-standing statement that clearly distinguishes racism from other forms of discrimination.

The parallels with sexism, class inequalities, bullying, heterosexism and the treatment of people with disabilities or individual learning needs are vitally important and need to be acknowledged. Only if **your policy addresses discrimination in all its forms** will you avoid polarisation or the divisive notion that some '-isms' are taken more seriously than others. The fact that there are many other forms of discrimination to be tackled should not, however, be allowed to detract from the message that racism has its own unique history and expression – and calls for its own very specific responses.

■ 2.4 What should our policy look like?

There are many innovative ways of expressing an institution's intentions in a policy, and no rigid rules about structuring or presenting them. Nevertheless, most policies tend to follow this fairly standard format.

A standard EO/AR policy usually includes:

❏ A GENERAL POLICY STATEMENT linked to the school's mission, that sets out the principles and practices your school is committed to in its main areas of operation – for example

BRIXHAM SCHOOL
EQUAL OPPORTUNITIES STATEMENT

- The community we serve is, in social and ethnic terms, very mixed. We believe this enriches the life and work of the school and we are committed to meeting the educational challenges this presents.

- We are opposed to racism, stereotyping and all other forms of discrimination based on a person's class, ethnic origin, gender, age, nationality, language, religion, disability, sexuality or size.

- We believe that every pupil should be actively encouraged to have a positive self-image; to achieve to their full ability; and to treat others with fairness and respect.

- Our aim is to reflect this in the way our school is staffed, the lessons and subjects we teach, the out-of-school activities we organise, the learning support we provide and our relationship with parents, employers and local community groups.

❑ A series of more detailed policy statements that give the reasons for having a policy in each area and specify your broad objectives – for example

---

How our school is staffed (Staff Recruitment):

So as to guarantee that all our students can achieve to the best of their ability, we are committed to recruiting the very best teachers from backgrounds and communities similar to their own, and to providing all staff with opportunities to develop themselves both personally and professionally. We will do this by

- Making a commitment to Equal Opportunities and opposition to racism a condition of service

- Providing induction and regular professional development opportunities (etc)...

These individual policy objectives form the basis for **a school-wide Action Plan** incorporating specific targets or initiatives for each key area; and for **departmental Action Plans** that spell out in detail how each department intends to deliver aspects of the policy in practical terms (See Unit 3, Action Planning).

■ 2.5 What are the 'ingredients' of an effective policy?

There is no magic formula for turning your school's good intentions into practice, but the most effective policy is one that is...

❑ 'OWNED' in the sense that **it has been discussed, developed or reviewed by those who are expected to implement it**

❑ CREDIBLE in that **it is seen as realistic and achievable by staff, parents and students**

❑ 'LIVE' in the sense that **It actively informs the day-to-day life and work of the school**

❑ ACCESSIBLE in that **it is easy to understand and appropriate for different audiences and uses**

In practice, this means that it should be the outcome of a regular school-wide debate in which everyone – students, parents, staff and governors – has an opportunity and is encouraged to have their say. This is most likely to happen if your policy has certain essential ingredients and is made available in a language and format that is 'user-friendly'.

Use the following checklists to 'quality assure' your new or existing EO/AR policy and identify ways of making it more lively and accessible. You may find that your policy meets all the relevant criteria, particularly if it is already well established and regularly reviewed. If not, the checklists should draw your attention to any shortcomings or ambiguities and help to highlight areas that may have been overlooked or neglected.

Different people may have very different ideas about what the policy should say, depending on their role and status in the school. It is important to hear everyone's views if you want to get a true picture. The School Council can play an important role in this. Remember to keep a record of any new ideas or suggestions and refer back to them when moving on to develop your Action Plan.

11

■ 2.6 CHECKLIST: WHO OWNS OUR POLICY?

Your aim here is to establish whether your school's EO/AR policy has been discussed, developed and/or reviewed by everyone who is expected to support and implement it – not just staff and students, but also parents, caretakers, administration and catering staff, cleaners and others who provide school-based services. Use this checklist to explore where people are in their thinking about EO/AR issues and to establish whether there is general 'ownership' of the policy.

Would you say that...	✔
The school's EO/AR policy represents the views of most... • teaching staff? • non-teaching or support staff? • managers? • parents? • students? • governors?	
Staff know the history of the school's EO/AR policy and how it was developed?	
Staff are introduced to the school's EO/AR policy during induction/ staff training/ another appropriate contexts and understand what it requires of them and others?	
Students are introduced to the school's EO/AR policy in induction/ tutorials/ PSE/ another appropriate context and understand their rights and responsibilities in this area?	
Staff, students and parents have been consulted about what the policy should say?	
The policy has a noticeable influence on the attitudes and behaviour of staff? students? parents? managers? service providers?	
Colleagues are generally comfortable discussing EO/AR issues and concerns with each other? with students? with managers?	
The school's EO/AR policy actively informs the day-to-day life and work of the school?	
The school's EO/AR policy is regularly reviewed and updated and used to identify school-wide objectives and targets?	

■ 2.7 CHECKLIST: WHAT DO PEOPLE THINK ABOUT OUR POLICY?

Which 3 comments about your school's EO Policy – or EO policies in general – are most likely to be expressed by... (a) staff? (b) students? (c) parents? (d) managers? (e) governors?	✔ a	✔ b	✔ c	✔ d	✔ e
It's about equal treatment for everyone					
It's anti-white					
It's a legal formality or requirement					
It's just a piece of paper – it doesn't change anything					
It makes people afraid to speak their mind					
It's about making sure everyone has equal access to services					
It's about 'political correctness'					
It's about making the very best use of human resources					
It gives everyone a fairer chance when applying for jobs					
It leads to conflict					
It's about social justice					
Black people benefit from it – but nobody else does					
It shows that the school takes a stand against racism					
It encourages black people to play the 'race card'					
It's about meeting people's individual needs					
It's a lot of hot air					

What does all this tell you about the status of your EO/AR policy? Compare your responses and use them to establish whether there is a need to revive or rejuvenate your existing policy, or develop a new one from scratch. The benefit of the latter approach is that it can be used to initiate widespread discussion and consultation, involving the whole school in a lively debate about what the EO/AR should say – and how it could be achieved.

■ 2.8 CHECKLIST: IS OUR POLICY CREDIBLE?

This checklist will help you to establish whether the commitments made in your school's EO/AR policy are seen as credible – i.e. realistic and achievable – by those who are expected to implement and adhere to it. This is best done by asking yourself HOW this is to be achieved in practice. Compare your responses and use them to explore the overall credibility of your policy. Then move on to discuss how you might amend or expand each clause to ensure that each of them can be delivered in practice.

DO WE HAVE A POLICY THAT ...	✔	HOW IS THIS ACHIEVED?
Opposes racism and all other forms of discrimination?		
Commits the school to working towards equality of access, provision and treatment for all staff and students, regardless of their race, culture, language, nationality, religion and other differences?		
Promotes friendship, co-operation and mutual understanding between students from different ethnic groups and social or religious backgrounds?		
Commits staff to delivering a curriculum that raises students' awareness of cultural, social, historical, political and community issues and encourages positive attitudes towards difference and diversity?		
Acknowledges the value of positive images of non-European cultures, contributions and achievements both in the school, the local community and beyond?		
Commits the staff to liasing closely with parents, local community groups and other relevant agencies to develop ways of combating racially-motivated violence and other unacceptable behaviour by young people both in and out of school?		
Provides for regular staff training on issues of racism, equal opportunities and ethnic diversity?		
Requires all staff to support this policy as an essential condition of service?		
Requires all students to conduct themselves in a way that complements this policy and supports an ethos of equality and respect for difference?		
Clearly outlines the procedures and sanctions that apply if staff or students do not adhere to the requirements of the policy?		
Promotes staff recruitment practices and other actions designed to ensure that the school's staff is representative of the young people and communities it serves?		
Commits the school to pupil surveys, consultation with parents and other consultative mechanisms to help highlight concerns or poor practice?		
Prohibits the use of school premises by individuals or organisations wishing to promote racist views or activities?		
Includes or refers to a detailed plan for implementing the above and reviewing progress on a regular and systematic basis?		

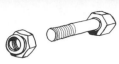

■ 2.9 IS OUR POLICY ACCESSIBLE?

There's little point in having a policy that no-one can understand because it is too long-winded or is written in a language few people use. Use this checklist to establish how accessible your policy really is. Then move on to discuss any SUGGESTIONS you may have for making it more 'user-friendly'.

IS OUR POLICY...	✔
Written in a language that is easy to understand?	
Accessible in terms of its layout, headings, format, print-size etc?	
Available to parents and students in the relevant community languages and in alternative formats (e.g. on cassette) where required?	
Concise – or available to parents and students in a summarised form?	
Jargon-free?	
In tune with all areas and aspects of school provision?	
Regularly discussed by governors, managers, staff, students and parents?	
Generally understood by governors, managers, staff, students and parents?	
Actively supported by managers and governors?	
A fair reflection of the school's overall mission and its strategic plans?	
Supported by the necessary resources – for example, a responsible senior manager, good quality teaching resources and funds for staff training?	
Linked to an achievable action plan that clearly identifies who is responsible for each task or objective?	
Linked to a realistic timeframe for both short and long-term implementation?	
Regularly monitored, reviewed and updated by everyone who has a stake in the school's reputation and achievements?	
Suggestions:	

UNIT 3: Turning Policy into Practice

OUTCOMES

Completing this Unit will help your school turn its policy into practice by means of ...

✔ a school-wide working party or focus group leading a whole-school response

✔ a pragmatic, step-by-step approach

✔ an explicit agenda and realistic aims

✔ consultation, debate and regular two-way communication

When involving others in discussions about the policy, this Unit will also help to ensure that...

✔ the aims and desired outcomes of all consultation meetings and other policy-related discussions are explicit

✔ the results of monitoring and any consultations, surveys or questionnaires are fed back in an interesting and engaging way

✔ discussion of the policy is integrated into the school's existing planning, evaluation and review cycle

In the most successful schools, the senior management team make it clear that the under-performance of any group is not acceptable, gather evidence systematically and challenge individuals and departments to spell out what they intend to do to improve the situation. Raising the Attainment of Minority Ethnic Pupils, OFSTED, 1999

■ 3.1 Creating the climate for change

Given the pace and extent of change in schools since the late 1980s, teachers are understandably weary of endless reform. Unless convinced of the need for change, colleagues are likely to be resistant to new initiatives – particularly if they do not stem from statutory requirements. Turning your new or existing policy into a consistent, whole-school practice therefore requires **a pragmatic approach** when developing or reviewing its policy.

Whilst the active support of the Headteacher and the commitment of a one or two key individuals will make a real difference to your progress, the research suggests that a collective approach involving **a school-wide working party or focus group** is more likely to bring about real and lasting change. Establishing a small, representative group that can drive the process ensures that there is a focal point for the work and a sense of whole-school responsibility for taking it forward.

Antiracism describes **a whole-school response** and therefore begs for whole-school involvement. However, staff and parents cannot be forced to alter their language or their thinking, nor can long-standing practices, attitudes or procedures be changed overnight. Your agenda for change will need to take account of this by adopting **an incremental or step-by-step approach** that builds on small, achievable changes rather than sudden or sweeping reforms; and by building in the necessary time for people to explore

their views, confront any fears and adapt to new ways of working. The action plan stemming from your new or existing policy will provide a blueprint for this process.

■ 3.2 Who should drive the policy development process?

The group that takes a lead in driving the policy development process and overseeing its implementation does not need to be large, nor does it need to be fully versed in all the issues. Its success in turning your school's policy into practice is likely to depend on a number of other, equally important factors, some of which are external and therefore not easy to control. All focus groups of this kind benefit from **the support of someone with power** – preferably the Headteacher, or where this is not available, that of a Governor, influential parents or a local Councillor.

The group also needs members who are committed to the work and prepared to give time and energy to taking it forward. **An explicit agenda and realistic aims** will help to keep people focused, but they will need protected time if they are to meet regularly and communicate effectively with others.

It will also help if the members of your EO/AR focus group have...

- ❏ patience in the face of cynicism, resistance or open opposition
- ❏ sensitivity to the dangers of polarisation
- ❏ the ability to differentiate between symbolic and real change
- ❏ a readiness to engage the whole school community in discussions about how to implement the policy
- ❏ the confidence to challenge bad practice or prevailing stereotypes and suggest constructive alternatives
- ❏ the capacity to influence every department
- ❏ the representation needed to cover or access all aspects of school life

In schools where teamwork and **an open, consultative approach to decision-making is** encouraged, the conditions will already be in place for taking this work forward. In others, the initial success of the group is more likely to dependant on the backing of the Headteacher or a sympathetic governor; and on winning **the support of students and parents**, who can exert a powerful influence if they know the arguments.

■ 3.3 Handling resistance

As with most policies, the *'what?'* tends to be far easier than the *'how?'* People are generally resistant to change unless convinced that it is necessary. Some colleagues may react defensively at the prospect of having to rethink their approach to the curriculum or their perceptions of students and parents. Others may be unhappy at the prospect of more work or feel uncomfortable with the term 'racism'. Whatever your colleagues' response, there will be less resistance if there is **consultation, debate and regular two-way communication** with those who are required to implement changes or new procedures. Openness and transparency in these discussions are more likely to result in consensus about what action is needed. A consultative approach involving discussions, surveys and invitations to comment will also encourage ownership of the outcomes by students and parents, although they may first need to be convinced that their views will be heard. Voluntary involvement, the choice of anonymity and a readiness to address any hidden agendas will also help.

■ 3.4 Avoiding 'overkill'

One of the most difficult questions when developing your EO/AR policy is how much time and attention to give it, taking account of the many other urgent priorities. Time is a shrinking resource, and people will resent you wasting theirs by organising meetings where their opinions are not valued or the outcomes are not made explicit.

Although you want your policy to be taken seriously, it is important to avoid 'overkill' – the feeling that it is being pushed onto people by zealots or given excessive attention at the expense of other, equally important issues. The most effective way of combating overkill is by

- ✔ making sure that the process of developing, implementing and reviewing your policy is as transparent as possible by explaining the intended benefits to all and what will be done with people's responses and suggestions

- ✔ planning in advance so that **the aims and desired outcomes of all consultation meetings and other policy-related discussions are explicit** and clearly linked to the development, evaluation or review of the policy

- ✔ ensuring that **the results of monitoring and any consultations, surveys, or questionnaires are fed back in an interesting and engaging way**, so that staff and students can see that their input was valued and acted upon, and feel some ownership of the results

- ✔ ensuring that **discussion of the policy is part of the school's existing planning, evaluation and review cycle**, not treated as a 'bolt-on' consideration that is unrelated to the day-to-day work of the school

The dangers of overkill are well documented. People resent messages that are 'rammed down their throats' without prior discussion, and they will resist initiatives that seem irrelevant or incidental to their 'real' work. There are a number of practical steps that can help to raise the profile of antiracism and embed it as standard good practice in your school, without invoking this response.

By far the best approach to antiracism is to make it intrinsic to everything your school does. This means integrating the discourse about what it should mean in practice into your strategic and operational planning, your quality assurance and self-assessment activities, your staff training and induction programme, staff meetings, assemblies, tutorials and lessons in such a way that it eventually becomes firmly embedded into the life and fabric of the school.

■ 3.5 CHECKLIST: ESTABLISHING A FOCUS GROUP

The checklist below suggests some of the success factors that your school's Equal Opportunities/ Anti-racist working party or focus group should be aiming for as it establishes its presence and influence in the school.

If such a group is already established, use the checklist to structure your early discussions, to review your achievements to date or to explore the conditions needed to drive the antiracist process forward.

If such a group has yet to be formed or is at an early stage in its development, use the checklist to identify possible members or to inform your deliberations about how the group will function, what outcomes it should work towards and whom it should be answerable to.

Do we have...	✔
A committed (and preferably voluntary) membership?	
Active support from the Headteacher or a sympathetic governor?	
One or two members who are sufficiently aware of the issues?	
Adequate resources to support staff and curriculum development?	
Clear ground-rules?	
Transparent procedures?	
Realistic aims?	
Consensus about how to achieve them?	
Allocated time to discuss issues and explore priorities?	
A consultative approach to decision-making?	
Opportunities to raise colleagues' awareness in meetings and training events?	
Members (or access to advisors, external trainers or community representatives) who can present the rationale for good practice in a clear and convincing way?	
Other success criteria?	

■ 3.6 CHECKLIST: MAKING ANTI-RACISM 'A PART OF EVERYTHING WE DO'

This checklist will help you to identify ways of 'embedding' antiracism in the life and work of your school. Begin by identifying the strategies that you think would work best and giving some thought to your reasons. Not all of the strategies listed here will suit your particular school, but you may be able to think of others that would. Move on to discuss how you would introduce them and what resources you would need.

Which of these strategies would work best in our school?	✔	How?	Resources needed?
Making responsibility for promoting and adhering to the policy an essential condition of service and including this in all **job descriptions**			
Including explicit antiracist criteria in **staff appraisals and classroom observation**			
Ensuring that the **induction of new staff** includes the rationale for the policy and explains how they are responsible for implementing it			
Producing all **memos and internal communications** about racism and related themes on a bright, easily identified colour			
Including a standard or regular feature on antiracism (achievements, initiatives, debates, etc) in the **school newsletter** and **communications with students and parents**			
Ensuring that the school prospectus, publicity and information about the school and all **external communications** include a statement highlighting the school's commitments in this area			
Including 'AR/equality implications?' as a standing item on all agendas including **departmental, governing body, working party and school committee meetings**			
Requiring departments to analyse the **performance and attainment of ethnic minority students** and, where necessary, to identify measures to address under-achievement			
Organising or promoting **regular staff development** to promote awareness and good practice			
Encouraging black/ethnic minority staff, students and parents who wish to contribute more actively to decision-making			
Establishing a consultative forum or mechanism for black and ethnic minority students to speak openly about any needs or concerns they may have			
Supporting an annual public or school-wide event that celebrates diversity and focuses attention on the importance of antiracism			
Other strategies?			

20

UNIT 4: Action Planning Strategies

OUTCOMES

Completing this Unit will help you to develop a strategic approach to implementing your EO(AR) policy. In particular, it will encourage you to ensure that...

✔ EO/AR objectives, targets and initiatives are the end result of a process of consultation

✔ the objectives and targets derived from your policy are PRECISE, ACHIEVABLE and TIMED

✔ staff are able to distinguish between what is essential in the short term and what is desirable in the long term

✔ whole-school ownership is encouraged by involving all sections of the school community

✔ termly and annual review dates are integrated into the school calendar and complement existing priorities

✔ qualitative feedback from students, parents and staff is given the same weight and attention as numerical evidence of 'success'

✔ questionnaires, debates, presentations and structured discussions in assemblies, tutorials, School Council and other forums ensure that all students have a way of making their views heard

It has become ever more evident ...that antiracism in symbolic gestures is meaningless and can reinforce racism. If the school does not involve the total community, teachers, ancillary staff, students and parents, both black and white, in the efforts to tackle racism in school, the whole exercise will end in failure.
Murder in the Playground; the Burnage Report, Macdonald et.al 1989

■ 4.1 What does Action Planning involve?

You may have reached agreement about what your Policy should say and how you will create the necessary conditions for its implementation, but the task is not complete until you have considered what your objectives will mean in practical terms. This involves discussing and completing a detailed, school-wide Action Plan that addresses five key questions:

❏ **WHAT** exactly does each objective mean in practice?

❏ **HOW** will we achieve this?

❏ **WHO** will be responsible for seeing that it happens?

❏ **WHEN** will we be ready to evaluate or review what we've achieved?

❏ **WHICH** criteria will tell us whether we are making progress?

If you give adequate time and consideration to each of these questions, your EO/AR policy will serve as a dynamic blueprint for change and development. If you don't, it is likely to sit in a filing cabinet somewhere and gather dust!

Your EO/AR agenda should be the outcome of a genuine process of consultation. If you have achieved this, departmental plans will flow naturally from your school-wide action plan by mirroring its objectives and 'picking up and running' with the relevant targets.

■ 4.2 Setting Objectives and Targets (WHAT?)

Your policy will probably include a number of broad objectives relating to different areas of school provision – for example, the Curriculum, Staff Recruitment, Language Provision, Behaviour etc. You may also have identified a need for specific actions in response to an internal self-assessment or an OFSTED inspection. To turn these objectives into specific targets or goals, individuals or groups representing the whole school community will need time to **explore in detail what each objective might mean in practice**.

When doing this, it is helpful to make a clear distinction between the broad objectives you set yourself and the specific or measurable targets you want to achieve.

Objectives and Targets: some examples

Objectives tend to describe clearly-defined, achievable actions or initiatives – for example

✔   to review the school's library and learning resources

✔   to develop improved referral procedures for students requiring EAL support in Year 7

✔   to organise a staff development workshop to raise awareness of the needs of travellers

Targets, on the other hand, refer to specific, measurable changes that are to be achieved over an agreed period – for example

✔   a specified increase in the number of EAL students who achieve GCSE Grades A*-C by September 2002

✔   a specified decrease in the number of African-Caribbean boys who are permanently excluded by July 2003

✔   a specific increase in the retention or attainment of children from travelling communities

The objectives you set will usually suggest specific targets and success criteria. For example, if one of the objectives listed in your Action Plan is **to organise a staff development workshop** to raise awareness of the needs of travellers, your (quantitative) target might be **80% attendance**, while your success criteria might include, in the short term, **a high level of satisfaction with the way the workshop was delivered** and, in the long term, **evidence of improved provision** for children from the local traveller community.

■ 4.3 Implementing Objectives and Targets (HOW?)

Your Equal Opportunities/Antiracist policy will be much easier to realise if your **objectives and targets are the end result of a process of consultation** with those who are expected to achieve them. The task will also prove more manageable if **the objectives and targets derived from your policy are PRECISE, ACHIEVABLE and TIMED**.

For example, if one of your policy objectives is...

> '*to make opposition to racism and support for equal opportunities a condition of service for all staff*'

...this could be expressed as a number of specific actions or activities. The 'how?' might involve...

✔   Organising a series of staff development events to raise awareness of the new policy and provide a forum staff to discuss key issues

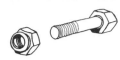

✔ Reviewing shortlisting criteria for all new posts

✔ Arranging a targeted workshop for staff and governors involved in staff interviews or appraisals

✔ Amending interviews to include an appropriate question for all candidates

✔ Developing explicit criteria for use in staff appraisals and classroom observations

You may find that you and your colleagues would like the school to be able to do everything listed here, yet have to accept frustrating compromises. It helps if **staff are able to distinguish between what is essential in the short term and what is desirable in the long term**. If a lack of time, staff or money is your school's main obstacle (and not just an excuse for inaction) focus on the activities or initiatives that are not too costly or resource-intensive and identify those that can be integrated into existing practices and procedures in the short term; then make plans to apply for the necessary funding – for example, from the Ethnic Minority Achievement Grant or SRB funding – so that you can plan to achieve this particular goal over a longer period.

Whatever the long-term vision of what could be accomplished in your school, a degree of realism is called for. Antiracism describes a process that is incremental and in this context, small achievable steps can be as important as large ambitious strides.

■ 4.4 Taking Responsibility (WHO?)

The school may be dependent on a few individuals for guidance and direction but they should not end up doing the bulk of the work! Where a plan's successful implementation relies solely on the energy of one or two key people, there is a risk of complacency and a real danger of having to start over if they decide to move on.

Where responsibility for EO/AR work is left to black and other ethnic minority staff, the risk increases. Although they may be an invaluable resource, there can be no grounds for assuming that your black colleagues will have the energy or expertise to take this work forward. Ideally, you should aim for an Action Plan that relies on school-wide involvement and includes widely delegated or rotating responsibilities from which everyone, regardless of their status or background, can learn.

Despite the limitations on people's time, you can ensure that **whole-school ownership is encouraged by involving all sections of the school community**. Some of the actions arising from your policy may need to be mandatory – for example, adhering to certain procedures or attending staff induction – but most will rely on voluntary co-operation and a degree of good will. If you take account of people's current workload and extra-curricular commitments, you are more likely to see results.

You may not manage to persuade everyone to engage with the issues, but even discussing someone's objections to a particular initiative or requirement can raise their awareness, if handled sensitively. Attempting to involve everyone may be unrealistic and could prove a recipe for disaster. Nevertheless, everyone should have a voice and a way of making their views and suggestions heard. Here the role of the School Council and of personal tutors is vital. The use of **questionnaires, debates, presentations and structured discussions in assemblies, tutorials, School Council and other forums ensures that all students have a way of making their views heard**. However, their comments and feedback will need to be sensitively handled, and staff may need training in order to feel confident in this role.

■ 4.5 Agreeing a time-frame (WHEN?)

Agreeing a realistic time-frame for implementing the different objectives and reviewing your progress with specific targets is an essential function of action planning. Words like 'on-going' have no place in the 'WHEN' column of your school-wide and departmental plans.

Deciding when to look back at your achievements and assess your progress to date should be relatively straightforward if evaluation and review activities are taken seriously in your school. A quality review cycle that is tied to the school calendar and to its three-year development plan will already be in place, and staff and students will have clearly-defined roles to play in the quality assurance process. Where this is not the case, HODs should **establish termly or annual review dates that complement existing priorities**. There is clearly little point in scheduling the review of a major EO/AR policy initiative during a week when all the key players are up to their ears in SATs.

Departmental and school-wide Action Plans should be reviewed annually, although individual initiatives and one-off activities may call for more immediate or regular appraisal.

■ 4.6 Agreeing success criteria (WHICH?)

Agreeing success criteria in advance will help you to ascertain whether you are making genuine progress. An invaluable tool for action-planning purposes, they help you to establish how you will know you've achieved what you set out to do. Individual success criteria could describe something relatively small and achievable – for example, the anticipated benefits of organising an assembly or display of work based around a particular theme; or they could help you to aim for something more ambitious, such as the desired changes in attitude resulting from a new policy or curriculum initiative.

■ 4.7 Developing and using Performance Indicators

Performance indicators are success criteria that provide you with a quantitative basis for 'measuring' your school's progress. This is a vital activity, both when reviewing existing EO/AR targets and when setting new ones. They do this by anticipating an increase, decrease or change that is in some way measurable.

For example, a school that is concerned about the under-achievement of African-Caribbean boys at GCSE might develop a number of strategies designed to achieve *a 10% increase year by year in the number of African-Caribbean boys achieving five or more GCSE grades A-C* over the coming three-year period. 'How' strategies might include a peer mentoring scheme or establishing ways of supporting and tracking the progress of named individuals who are at risk of under-achieving. In this case, the desired 10% increase serves as a useful performance indicator which, if compared from one year to the next, should give the school a clear indication of how successful it has been to date in meeting this target.

If student achievement rates are carefully monitored from the outset, this 10% figure (however ambitious) will serve as a useful annual performance indicator in its own right. However, such figures tend to be arbitrary and over-ambitious, unless they relate to national benchmarks and local data such as the performance of this group at GCSE both nationally and locally in comparable schools.

■ 4.8 How to use benchmarks

Benchmarks enable you to look beyond the school gates and compare your school's performance against a set of national, regional or local base-line figures. They provide managers and staff with the means to:

- ❑ argue the case for positive or remedial action and other EO/AR initiatives

- ❑ 'measure' key aspects of the school's performance by comparing internal and external data

- ❑ set performance and attainment targets that are in line with national, regional and/or local trends

- ❑ assess the significance of the school's achievements, including the attainment of identified ethnic minority groups

Many different organisations are involved in collecting the kind of data that can be used for benchmarking purposes. Possible sources include:

- • *DfEE*   *national SATs and GCSE achievement rates for identified groups of students, including ethnic minorities*

- • *LEAs*   *local/regional achievement rates*
  school exclusion rates

- • *research organisations*   *National Foundation for Educational*
  for analysis of census   *Research (NFER)*
  data, national/local   *Advisory Centre for Education (ACE)*
  findings and other   *Runnymede Trust*
  statistical data – e.g.

- • *CRE (Education)*   *data relating to discriminatory practices in schools*

- • *ATL, NUT, NAS-*   *data relating to the recruitment and*
  UWT   *treatment of black/ other ethnic minority staff*

Collecting and analysing such data for benchmarking purposes can seem unnecessarily time-consuming, but it doesn't have to be. For example, it can be made more manageable by including some of the tasks in your school's Maths, Social Science, IT or PSE curriculum. This has the added benefit of encouraging students' involvement, developing their key skills and giving them a stake in the target-setting process. Like the results of surveys and in-house monitoring, careful thought needs to be given to the way the information is interpreted, presented and used.

■ 4.9 Reviewing and evaluating progress

Discussing your progress with team or departmental action plans provides an ideal opportunity to invite colleagues to review your existing targets and give some feedback on what is helping or hindering them from meeting the school's policy commitments and the EO/AR objectives in your school-wide action plan.

Exploring common goals and evaluating achievements encourages transparency and a shared sense of mission, and most people will appreciate why it is important. They will also appreciate the opportunity to take stock of their progress and agree what else needs to be done. Where this is not the case, managers may have to actively sell the idea that doing this now could prevent unnecessary frustration, heartache or conflict in future.

■ 4.10 AGREEING PERFORMANCE INDICATORS: A MEASURE OF OUR SUCCESS?

The following list provides some examples of performance indicators used by schools and LEAs. With some relevant national or local benchmarks and your school's EO/AR action plan in front of you, use it to develop your own list of performance indicators, along with any other criteria to help you measure your success.

Start by identifying the performance indicators (PIs) that are most relevant to your school and its context, then discuss each one in detail. You could do this by addressing the following questions:

❑ Which particular target or objective in our action plan would this PI relate to?

❑ What level of reduction or improvement would we like to see?

❑ Can we express this as a percentage?

❑ Is this figure realistic? (How does it relate to local/national benchmarks)?

❑ What would this information tell us about the progress we have made towards meeting the commitments in our EO/AR policy?

EO/AR PERFORMANCE INDICATORS: A LIST OF EXAMPLES

❑ Participation rates for ethnic minority students in areas of the curriculum where they are over- or under-represented

❑ Exclusion rates for identified groups

❑ Pupil attainment and achievement rates

❑ The range and diversity of employers providing work experience placements

❑ Levels of absenteeism among students from a particular ethnic minority group

❑ The number of incidents recorded in the school's racial incidents book

❑ Student satisfaction rates with how aspects of the EO/AR policy are delivered

❑ Appointment and promotion rates for ethnic minority staff

❑ Staff participation rates in EO/AR training

❑ Parent participation rates in parents' evenings and other relevant activities

■ 4.11 ACTION PLANNING: An Example

Policy objective:	Actions to : be taken	Who will be responsible	Deadline/ review dates	Success criteria/ PIs
'To make opposition to racism and support for equal opportunities an essential condition of service for all new and existing staff'	• 2 HR WORKSHOPS TO RAISE AWARENESS OF OUR REVISED EO/AR POLICY (ALL STAFF REQUIRED TO ATTEND) + INDUCTION SESSION FOR ALL NEW STAFF – How will we use it? – What are the practical implications for each of us?	• Sue D. (Staff Devt. Co-ordinator) to set dates and organise in liaison with Head	By Sept 2001	All staff(100%) will have taken part in a relevant event 80% of all written evaluations show the event was considered useful
	• 2HR SESSION FOR GOVERNORS/ HODs/ STAFF WHO INTERVIEW – What Qs should we be asking? – What skills/ experience should we be looking for?	• Sue D. to circulate the suggestions to EO/AR W/Party	By July 2000	Review of interviews (via minutes) will show this Q. is now more meaningfully addressed
	• REVIEW 'ESSENTIAL' CRITERIA USED FOR SHORT-LISTING AND REVISE INTERVIEW QUESTION(S)	• EO/AR W/Party	By end of April 2000	Revised criteria and more meaningful (standard) interview question
	• DEVELOP APPROPRIATE CRITERIA FOR INCLUSION IN ALL STAFF PROBATIONS, APPRAISALS and CLASSROOM OBSERVATIONS	• Headteacher, in liaison with EO/AR W/PARTY	Annually, in May	Annual feedback from HODs via departmental annual reports.

27

■ 4.12 ACTION PLANNING: A WHOLE-SCHOOL APPROACH

Working with others in your department or team, apply the five key action-planning questions (WHAT? HOW? WHO? WHEN? WHICH?) to each of the objectives in your school's Equal Opportunities (Anti-racist) policy and use the responses to help you develop a school-wide or departmental Action Plan (as appropriate), using the example provided. Begin each statement in the 'how?' column with **an action verb** to ensure that the activity involves carrying out a specific task – i.e. a task that is potentially 'do-able'. Try to avoid verbs like 'to enable, to ensure, to explore' etc. unless they describe a precise activity. Your school-wide/ departmental action plan is only complete when each task is accompanied by the name of the person(s) responsible for co-ordinating and monitoring it and a date by which you expect to be able to review your progress and achievements.

DEPARTMENT/TEAM   **DATE**

WHAT? (Policy Objectives)	HOW? (Specific Actions)	WHO? (Named Resonsibility)	WHEN? (Deadlines for Completion/Review)	WHICH? (Success Critieria)

UNIT 5: Monitoring for Change

OUTCOMES

Completing this unit will encourage you to think of the many practical ways monitoring can be used to support the objectives in your policy and ensure that it serves as a genuine vehicle for change by collecting data that

✔ provides an accurate social and ethnic profile of your school

✔ serves as a reference point when evaluating outcomes and achievements

✔ provides evidence of new or changing circumstances, statistical trends and patterns

✔ gives useful insights into the unwitting effects of institutional racism

It will also help you to ensure that

✔ the areas and categories used for monitoring purposes are relevant to departmental needs

✔ the interpretation of any quantitative data is verified, using a variety of qualitative methods

✔ you take full account of other considerations like students' gender or postcode, their entitlement to free school meals and individual learning needs.

A school is better equipped to offer each child suitable education if the basic facts about his or her cultural identity – including ethnic origin, linguistic background and religion – are known. DES Circular 16/89, July 1989

...It is in those schools with the best ethnic data that the performance of the minority ethnic students has improved most strongly... unless the performance of different ethnic groups in a wide range of school provision is monitored, it is impossible to be sure that appropriate and often scarce resources are being used to maximum effect. Raising the Attainment of Minority Ethnic Students, OFSTED, 1999

■ 5.1 Why does monitoring get a bad press?

Monitoring and the use and interpretation of data have been contentious issues in schools for many years. Ethnic monitoring in all schools was only formally re-introduced in 1990, after years of lobbying.[3] There remain some valid doubts about the value of official government categories[4] that have tended in the past to confuse 'race', ethnicity and nationality and may not reflect the social and ethnic complexity of many school populations, especially in urban areas.

Since 1992 when performance tables were first introduced, data on pupil achievement have been consistently misinterpreted by the media. It is often used to undermine public confidence in the work teachers do, sometimes in the most challenging of school environments. In the more sensationalised debates about 'league table' results, crude numerical data have been seized upon as 'evidence' of a school's standards or achievement, with little regard for the social context and learning needs of its students.

Monitoring is therefore typically seen as a tedious paper exercise that serves no practical purpose other than to satisfy DfEE requirements and to 'beat schools up' with. There is also some legitimate frustration with the emphasis on gathering quantitative data at the expense of – or as a poor substitute for – qualitative evidence. This is a valid concern, particularly where the collection of data is seen as an end in itself.

In their investigation into the attainment of minority ethnic students in schools, OFSTED found that, although schools are required to collect attainment data and analyse it according to ethnic group, 'few use this information as a key management tool for raising standards'. The report also confirmed the urgency of clear guidance from central government and LEA support by concluding that ' in many LEAs, there is an uncertainty bordering on helplessness about what are effective strategies to improve attainment for some groups'.

■ 5.2 The case for ethnic monitoring

Since January 1990, education authorities in England and Wales have been required to submit returns on the ethnic origins of school teachers, including information about pay, seniority and specialisation. This data can be used by schools to measure their success in attracting more ethnic minority teachers.

Since September 1990, all local authority schools have also had a statutory duty to collect ethnically-based data on their students. The information, which should ideally be supplied by parents on a voluntary basis during admissions interviews, relates to each child's

- ❏ ethnic origin
- ❏ language
- ❏ religious affiliation

The DfEE also requires returns to be made on

- ❏ examination results at age 16 and 18
- ❏ the destinations of students leaving school

If carefully analysed, this data can provide your school with invaluable information for planning and self-assessment purposes. The task may seem tedious, but having given time and energy to developing your EO/AR policy, and having collected the data for external (LEA or DfEE) consumption, it makes little sense to ignore its relevance to governors, staff and managers.

Quite apart from satisfying DfEE or LEA requirements, careful ethnic monitoring provides an information base that will allow you to keep a regular and systematic check on the progress of black children. It may also reveal trends or patterns suggesting discriminatory treatment or help you to identify needs that call for EMTAG (Ethnic Minority and Travellers Achievement Grant) funding or a strategic response.

Monitoring provides the statistical basis for **a social and ethnic profile of your school**, allowing you to see at a glance which communities it serves and how different categories of students are faring.

✔ It serves as **a reference point when evaluating outcomes and achievements**, particularly when used in conjunction with national benchmarks, LEA averages and school projections.

✔ It provides vital **evidence of new or changing circumstances** and alerts you to **statistical trends and patterns** that call for a planned or targeted response.

✔ It **can offer useful insights into the unwitting effects of institutional racism**.

Colleagues may first need to be convinced that the data they are being asked to collect and analyse will be used constructively, both to support their efforts and actively inform their deliberations. This is most likely to happen if **the areas and categories used for monitoring purposes are relevant to departmental needs** and if the instructions given to staff are clear.

Statistics are open to misinterpretation, and it is important to supplement them with other forms of evidence. If analysed and interpreted intelligently, they can reveal a lot – but they will rarely give you the full picture. It is vital that **your interpretation of any quantitative data is verified, using a variety of qualitative methods** such as tutor group and staff discussions, evaluations, feedback from the School Council, consultations with parents and community groups, suggestions boxes, impromptu playground surveys and any other innovative methods you can devise.

■ 5.3 COMMUNICATING THE NEED FOR DATA: A MEMO FROM THE HEAD

Memo

From: Headteacher
To: All HODs
Date: 22.10.99

Our efforts to monitor the progress of students by ethnicity and gender have highlighted concerns about under-achievement by certain groups, specifically white and African-Caribbean boys. GCSE results for this year are attached, and HODs are asked to comment on the following:

1. How do this year's results for this group compare with
   • the past three years?
   • national averages?
   • estimated grades?

2. Do the results highlight any significant differences in performance
   • by ethnicity?
   • by gender?
   • by teaching group?

3. If so, are you aware of any contributing factors?

4. Can you/ your staff suggest practical ways of redressing the differentials you have identified?

5. Please outline any resource or staff development implications

This information is needed by **1.10.01 latest**, and will be tabled for discussion at the next Governing Body meeting (Oct 29th).

■ 5.4 Deciding what to monitor

Because of the increasing complexity of school populations, deciding what to monitor can be a challenge in its own right. An awareness of students' social and religious backgrounds, their mixed ethnicity or transnational origins and their specific language and learning needs is rarely evident in schools that rely solely on DfEE recommended categories that were based on the 1991 census.

Ethnic groups are not homogenous and categorisations like 'Black-African' or 'black-other' may disguise important differences among students who appear, on paper at least, to be from the same ethnic background. This is equally true of the term 'White', which may include several ethnic or national minorities yet is typically assumed to be an all-embracing category. Even where the categories used are more appropriate, monitoring by ethnicity should never be regarded as a substitute for individual needs assessment; or for the learning that can result when form tutors really get to know their students on a one-to-one basis.

Clearly, a student's language, religion and ethnic origins are not the only considerations. Schools should be prepared to think carefully about the categories and sub-categories they use for monitoring purposes, and wherever appropriate they should **take account of other factors like students' gender or postcode, their entitlement to free school meals and individual learning needs.**

The academic achievement and post-school destinations of ethnic minority students is a legitimate government concern, but it is only one of a number of areas that your school should be scrutinising if you are genuinely concerned about institutional racism. Use the checklist and activities in this Unit to identify other areas your school may need to be monitoring on a regular basis – and what you could do with the data.

■ 5.5 DEVELOPING A WHOLE-SCHOOL PROFILE

Begin by reviewing the **social and ethnic categories** your school is currently using for monitoring purposes and deciding whether they are adequate.

How could the thirteen standard DfEE categories used throughout the 90s be developed to give a more accurate and meaningful profile of the staff and students in your school?

'White', for example, may well include significant numbers of Jewish, Welsh-speaking or Irish students or children whose parents are European refugees. This will have implications for the school's caterers (Kosher food?), librarians (Welsh-language books?), classroom teachers (more positive images of the Irish in the curriculum?) and others in the school.

Try doing the same kind of needs analysis for the following ethnic categories:

'White'?	Indian?	Asian-Other?
Black-Caribbean?	Pakistani?	Other-Other?
Black-African?	Bangladeshi?	
Black-Other?	Chinese?	

Census categories for 2001 will eventually provide schools and LEAs with new data that give greater insight into the needs of students. Study the proposed categories below and discuss whether there is any other data your school would need in order to provide managers, staff, parents and/or governors with a more accurate ethnic profile:

(a) **White**
   British   Irish
   Any other white background (please write in below)

(b) **Mixed**
   White and Black Caribbean   White and Black African   White and Asian
   Any other mixed background (please write in below)

(c) **Asian or Asian British**
   Indian   Pakistani   Bangladeshi
   Any other Asian background (please write in below)

(d) **Black or Black British**
   Caribbean   African
   Any other Black background (please write in below)

(e) **Chinese or other ethnic group**
   Chinese   Any other (please write in below)

How helpful would it be to have access to more detailed information about students' or parents' religious backgrounds? For example, what would the following religious categories tell you about the food, festivals, dress codes, obligations and attitudes your school needs to consider? And are there any categories missing?
   None
   Christian (incl. Church of England, Protestant and all other churches)
   Buddhist
   Hindu
   Muslim
   Sikh
   Jewish
   Any other religion (please write in below)

■ 5.6 CHECKLIST: WHAT SHOULD WE BE MONITORING?

Taking account of the commitments made in your EO(AR) policy – and the fact that academic achievement is only one of a number of possible success criteria – use the following checklist to prioritise the different **areas your school should be monitoring more closely**. You may want to amend the list or suggest other areas to include.

What should we monitor more closely...?	✔	How? (e.g. by postcode? Ethnicity? Gender? Eligibility for free school meals?))
Applications		
Admissions		
Attendance		
Examination results ...at GCSE ...at A level		
Other achievements?		
Fixed term/ permanent exclusions ...by nature of incident/ offence? ...staff/ others involved? ...staff responsible for decision(s) to exclude?		
Referrals to ...(e.g.) education psychology ...social services ...other agencies?		
Language/ additional learning support needs		
Post-school progression		
Subject choices/ options		
Racial incidents		
Staff appointments		
Staff promotions		
Any other areas?		

■ 5.7 Making data accessible

Monitoring has little point unless the information it provides is actively used to inform the life and work of the school by helping managers and staff to identify priorities, improvements and targets. Although many schools systematically collect data, the research suggests that few know what to do with it. The checklist below gives a number of possible uses of ethnic data. If you haven't already done so, you may want to consider whether now would also be a good time to introduce monitoring in other EO-related areas – for example, by gender or by eligibility for free school meals.

Chose one or more **areas that you are not yet monitoring** in your school and use these questions to explore how this could be achieved in practical terms:

❑   How will we access this information? Who will supply it?

❑   Who will collate it? Aggregate and analyse it? Circulate it?

❑   Who is best placed to interpret the data and explore its implications?

❑   What other evidence or feedback is needed to support it?

❑   How can we ensure that it is discussed by departments? Parents? Governors? Advisors? Other interested parties?

❑   How can the information be reproduced graphically or made more accessible?

❑   How else could the data be used to support our school's EO/AR policy and improve practices or achievements in areas of concern?

You may find it helpful to develop a **flowchart** showing the progress and various uses of the data from the point of collection onwards. If working with others, use a flipchart so that everyone can contribute.

Notes

3   The DES began collecting statistics on the numbers of 'immigrant' students in 1966, primarily to enable LEAs to make provision for students whose first language was not English but also to inform dispersal policies advocated by central government. The definition of 'immigrant' was problematic, however, and led to an underestimation of the number of black children in schools. In 1973, Margaret Thatcher recommended that the collection of ethnic data should cease. Calls for ethnic monitoring to be reintroduced fell on deaf ears until the recommendations of the Swann/Rampton Committee led to its reinstatement from September 1990.

4   The categories currently used by the DfEE are based on the ethnic group classifications used in the 1991 census: White, Black-African, Black-Caribbean, Black-Other, Indian, Pakistani, Bangladeshi, Chinese, Other-Asian, Other-Other. It is proposed that these categories should be changed for the 2001 Census to take account of religious, mixed and other backgrounds (See Activity 5.5). Revised categories proposed for the 2001 census will provide schools with a more useful ethnic profile. The proposed categories for England and Wales are listed in Activity 5.4.

■ 5.8 CHECKLIST: MONITORING FOR A PURPOSE?

How could we use the data we collect to...	Suggestions
analyse **pupil attainment**, including SATs, GCSE and A level results, by ethnic/ other group to identify groups that are under-achieving?	
track the **progress of individual students and groups** at whole school, department and/or subject level?	
compare **teachers' projections** with students' actual assessment results and use the results to address any evidence of low expectations?	
monitor **option choices** by ethnic group to identify any stereotypical patterns that suggest there is a need for earlier remedial action?	
monitor the school's **SEN register** to establish whether any (ethnic minority/other) group appears disproportionately?	
monitor the number of **racial incidents** in the school, including name-calling, racial taunting, fights etc?	
monitor the **movement between ability sets** of any ethnic groups that are under-achieving?	
monitor **students' attendance** and parents' **attendance at parents evenings** by ethnic group to identify whether there is a need for improved home-school liaison?	
monitor the cause, length and number of **permanent and fixed-term exclusions** by ethnic group to identify any implications for the school's behaviour policy?	
monitor the **take-up of study support** and other extra-curricular activities by ethnic group with a view to identifying unmet needs?	

UNIT 6: Improving Your School Environment

OUTCOMES

Completing this Unit will encourage you to think of practical ways of improving your school ethos and environment. In particular, it will help you to ensure that

✔ the school conveys the message that diversity is celebrated and racism is outlawed

✔ young people learn in an environment that prepares them to live in a multi-ethnic society

✔ there is an absence of racist (and other offensive) graffiti

✔ posters, art and displays of students' work featuring non-European themes are displayed in common areas

✔ a Code of Conduct that promotes respect for one another and for the environment is prominently displayed in classrooms, staffrooms and other common areas

✔ the school has a proactive response to antisocial behaviour that seeks to reduce conflict and promote interpersonal skills

✔ staff and students are at ease discussing diversity and antiracism, when issues arise

✔ students are given clear messages about acceptable behaviour, dress and language

✔ These changes are part of an on-going, strategic, school-wide response

37

There is such a thing as 'institutional body language' – messages (that) are given and received through an organisation's customs, procedures, rules (and) regulations... Inclusive schools, inclusive society, Race On the Agenda, Trentham Books, 1999

■ 6.1 Creating the right 'feel'

Your school can demonstrate its commitment to racial equality not just through what it says and does but also through how it looks and feels – its 'institutional body language'. This means moving beyond your declared policies and written procedures to consider what kind of impression students, parents and visitors receive when they walk into and around the school. The message you should be trying to convey is that, in this school at least, **diversity is celebrated and racism is outlawed** – in all its various forms.

Whether the ethnic composition of your school is predominantly 'white' or ethnically diverse the school has a responsibility to ensure that **young people learn in an environment that prepares them adequately for the multi-ethnic society in which they will live and work**. In other words, they need to see black, brown, red and yellow-skinned people in active, non-subservient roles, performing non-stereotypical activities and celebrating a range of different life achievements. This is equally true of women, people with disabilities and some of the other groups mentioned in your EO/AR policy.

■ 6.2 Transforming common areas

With a little forethought, the ethos of your school and the appearance of common areas can be radically transformed. For example, a sign saying 'would all visitors please report to reception' in the main community languages makes an immediate welcoming statement to everyone who walks into the school. Photographs of the staff, or images of students at work – particularly if they confirm the diversity of the school and its community – will make an equally important impression.

The **absence of racist graffiti**, and the prominent display of **posters, art and displays of students' work featuring non-European themes** speak volumes about the kind of school yours aspires to be. However, your efforts cannot be confined to what people can see on the walls. Such changes may challenge how people think, but they are likely to remain cosmetic unless supported by efforts to change how staff and students behave.

A school-wide **Code of Conduct that promotes mutual respect and tolerance** is a must. This involves developing **a proactive response to antisocial behaviour** such as name-calling or graffiti-writing; and engaging the whole school in a dialogue about what constitutes acceptable behaviour, based on students' personal experiences of being bullied, teased or harassed. Many schools develop Behaviour Policies for this purpose.

■ 6.3 Changing your school culture

There could never be a definitive tick-list for the kind of cultural changes schools may need to undergo in order to create **an ethos and environment in which staff and students are genuinely at ease with diversity and antiracism**. Nevertheless, there are countless schools around the country – around the world, in fact – where this has been achieved, suggesting that schools can change their ethos and culture, particularly if they embark on the task with the active support of staff, parents, students and managers.

When thinking about the culture that prevails in the staffroom, corridors or playground, think also about the other cultural influences that have helped to shape attitudes and behaviour outside school. Many young people, especially those from black or other ethnic minority backgrounds, will be juggling a number of conflicting expectations. This may be expressed in their language, clothing or possessions; in their attitudes towards others; in their assumptions about what it is to be male or female; or in their ways of handling conflict. Giving **clear messages about acceptable behaviour, dress and language** will help them to know what to bring with them into the school – and what to leave at the school gate.

■ 6.4 CHECKLIST: DEVELOPING THE RIGHT INSTITITUTIONAL 'BODY LANGUAGE'

Use this checklist to identify the changes that would improve the antiracist ethos in your school or change your institutional 'body language'. Where the suggested strategies seem inappropriate, substitute them with suggestions of your own.

Like the other ideas in this *Toolkit*, the suggestions in the following checklist will only work if they are part of **an on-going, strategic, school-wide response.**

Do we (or could we) have	✔
A whole-school Code of Conduct that outlaws racism, name-calling, bullying and other antisocial behaviour and promotes a safe, non-threatening learning environment? **An unambiguous antiracist message** conveyed through the prominent display of relevant posters and the school's Code of Conduct in classrooms, staffrooms and corridors?	
Teaching and non-teaching staff who reflect the ethnic diversity of the local community and society in general? **School governors** who are from ethnic minority backgrounds or aware of the issues and needs of local black/ ethnic minority communities? **Involvement by black/ethnic minority parents** in all aspects of the school's work and decision-making, including the governing body, parents evenings, fund-raising, careers guidance and appropriate classroom activities?	
Posters, exhibitions and other positive visual images of and by ethnic minorities, conveying diverse cultures, lifestyles, historical experiences and individual achievements? **Displays of students' work** that reflect relevant global/cultural/social/community/ environmental themes addressed across the curriculum? **Regular monitoring of common areas**, including notice-boards, toilets and changing rooms, to detect and remove offensive graffiti?	

Do we (or could we) have	
Signs and notices in the locally spoken languages, including directions, fire regulations, Health and Safety instructions etc. where required? **Community language announcements**, information to parents, articles in the school newsletters etc., where appropriate? **Access to professional interpreters** where needed eg. at parents evenings, disciplinary hearings?	
Library and learning resources such as newspapers, journals, magazines, software, resource packs and reference books that highlight events and issues relevant to black/ other ethnic minority communities? **Textbooks, novels and reference books** that refer to black/ other ethnic minority experiences, include black/ non-European role models and challenge stereotypes? **An inclusive curriculum** that is respectful of difference and exploits all opportunities to explore a variety of cultural and ethnic identities?	
Access to specialist staff including counsellors, EAL teachers, home-school liaison workers and mediators to support the needs of students from particular ethnic minority groups? **A mentoring, peer support, 'buddy' or mediation scheme** to support individual students at risk of exclusion or under-achievement?	

Do we (or could we) have	✔
A safe space offering sanctuary, advice and support to students who need help coping with angry feelings or 'school rage'? **Peer mediation schemes involving targeted groups of students who are trained to reduce, defuse and resolve conflict?** **Guidelines supported by regular staff training on how to resolve conflicts with or among students?**	
Canteen/school dinner menus offering a choice of meals and snacks that reflects the full range of students' religious/ ethnic tastes and dietary requirements? **Dress requirements and changing or prayer facilities** that take full account of students' religious obligations?	

Do we (or could we) have	✔
Assemblies, concerts and other multicultural events that feature folk music, anthems and popular songs from around the globe using traditional instruments and musicians? **Tutorials, outings, social and extra-curricular activities** that reflect a range of cultural interests?	
Community networks with relevant black/ ethnic minority organisations and businesses and contact with the local Community Relations Council? **Links with voluntary and community organisations** that meet the particular social, psychological, language or religious needs of black/ ethnic minority students, including asylum-seekers, learners of English as an additional language, young Muslims etc? **Contacts, partnerships and twinning arrangements** with schools, organisations and/or communities in Africa, Asia and Latin America?	
Explicit, well-publicised grievance procedures, linked to the school's behaviour policy and/or Code of Conduct? **Clear guidelines for parents and students** about the way all staff are expected to behave and how the school uses exclusions and other sanctions? **The right of students to complain about unfair treatment** and to appeal against extreme punishments and sanctions? **The right to be represented** at official hearings by an advocate; and to be heard by a representative panel that includes someone from their own ethnic group?	
Other suggestions?	

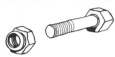

■ 6.5 CHALLENGING RACISM: HOW WELL DO WE RESPOND?

A whole-school Code of Conduct will only be effective if staff are confident to challenge unacceptable behaviour, attitudes and practices. A lot depends on the context and there is rarely only one way of responding to a situation. You can learn a good deal just from sharing your thoughts and fears with other colleagues. Working in pairs or a small group, discuss how you might respond in the following situations:

1   During parents evening, a parent refers to an Asian family walking past as a 'those Pakis'. They do not appear to have heard her comment – but you did.

2   A recently admitted Traveller is being subtly excluded by the children in your Year 8 Tutor Group. They are reluctant to sit next to her and she appears to have made no friends since her arrival several weeks ago.

3   You overhear a 14 year-old African-Caribbean boy calling his Asian friend 'coolie' in the playground one break time. The boy responds by calling him 'nigger'. They continue playing together and no offence appears to have been taken on either side.

4   During a review of school exclusion figures by the Governing Body, it becomes evident that over 40% of all fixed term and permanent exclusions over the past year have involved black (African-Caribbean) boys. One of the governors, a black parent, suggests this is evidence of institutional racism.

5   Your head of department insists on calling a Tamil student in your tutor group by an English name because she finds it 'easier to pronounce'.

6   A Muslim girl in Year 7 whose parents insist on her keeping her legs covered during PE and not taking communal showers, is being teased by other children. You overhear them telling her she 'stinks' and 'should take a bath'.

7   A group of black parents has written to the Headteacher suggesting that some areas of the curriculum are eurocentric and do not reflect the cultures and experiences of their children. They say they are particularly concerned about the way sciences are taught, and name a colleague who they say has dismissed their efforts to challenge this.

8   The only Kurdish child in the school, a 15 year old asylum seeker, has been missing classes for some time. When visited by a truancy officer, he claims he is scared to come to school because a group of boys has been calling him names and threatening to beat him up.

9   A boy in Year 9 has recently begun to make overtly racist comments and show off his swastika tattoo. Both his father and elder brothers are reputed to be active members of the BNP (British National Party).

10 An African-Caribbean girl suddenly becomes very ill one day at school and has to be rushed to hospital. You subsequently discover that she has Sickle Cell Anaemia. No one on the staff seems to have been aware of her condition, or the implications.

What similar situations have you witnessed or experienced where racism could have been a factor? And how did you respond?

41

How effectively you respond in such situations will largely depend on the context in which they arose. Other considerations will include

❑   How well you know the person(s) concerned

❑   Their status, and whether they have any power over you

❑   How confident you feel to make the necessary arguments

❑   How much support is available from colleagues and senior managers

Use the discussion you've had to draw up a list of good practice guidelines for inclusion in the Staff Handbook. If working with others, use a flipchart so that everyone can contribute their ideas and suggestions.

CHALLENGING AND INTERVENTION STRATEGIES: A CHECKLIST

Racist views, comments and assumptions are more commonplace in schools than most of us would like to think, and if we allow them to pass without comment, it gives licence and power to those who hold them. Use the following checklist to identify the challenging and intervention strategies that work best for you or your staff team. Try to recall the times when you have – or would like to have – used them.

You may want to record these incidents in the space provided and develop them as case studies that could be used in tutorials, staff training or staff/ student induction.

CHALLENGING STRATEGIES

- ✔ Avoid confrontation and aggression

- ✔ Respect the person's personal space, however much you disagree with their views

- ✔ Challenge the ideas – not the person

- ✔ Repeat the comment to check your understanding of it

- ✔ Ask the person to repeat themselves or explain what they mean

- ✔ Expose irrational or contradictory arguments by quoting the relevant research/ statistics/ counter-arguments/ historical context/ legislation etc.

- ✔ Use humour where appropriate

- ✔ Relate the issues to the person's class/age/gender/disability and try to find some parallels

- ✔ Raise your concerns in tutorials, departmental meetings or informal staffroom discussions or with senior managers, as appropriate

INTERVENTION STRATEGIES

- ✔ Listen carefully and get the full story before intervening

- ✔ Pay attention to body language and other signs

- ✔ Avoid taking sides and try to remain objective

- ✔ If necessary, diffuse the situation by separating the parties involved

- ✔ Empower victims by offering them support or advocacy

- ✔ Where appropriate, encourage witnesses/ other people to suggest an appropriate response

- ✔ Take firm, swift action in cases of violence, harassment, bullying or verbal abuse

UNIT 7: Staffing and Human Resources

OUTCOMES

Completing this unit will help to ensure that

✔ governors, managers and others responsible for the recruitment and selection of staff are trained to take full account of EO(AR) considerations, including the relevant legal and statutory requirements

✔ all applicants are required to demonstrate their awareness of EO issues and, where appropriate, their understanding of the needs of students from ethnic minority communities

✔ those involved in shortlisting or interviewing candidates understand the importance of adhering to fair, objective interviewing and selection criteria

✔ the school is committed to encouraging black and ethnic minority appointments at all levels within the organisation

✔ staff are regularly encouraged to discuss the EO(AR) issues that concern them and to work together to identify practical responses.

✔ the inclusion of EO/AR activities in all staff training and of 'race and other equalities implications' on all departmental/ committee agendas is seen as normal practice

■ 7.1 Staff recruitment and selection

With the exception of its students, the people who work in your school are its most precious resource. Since it is they who determine the success of your EO(AR) policy, careful thought needs to be given to the criteria used to select and appoint staff and the support and in-service training (INSET) they receive once in post.

EO(AR) principles should be integral to your school's recruitment and selection procedures. This is most likely to happen if **governors, managers and others responsible for the recruitment and selection of staff are trained to take full account of EO(AR) considerations, including the relevant legal and statutory requirements** (see Unit 1).

In particular, it is important that **those involved in shortlisting or interviewing understand the importance of adhering to fair, objective interviewing and selection criteria**, and asking questions based on the explicit requirements listed in the job specification. Where only one person is responsible for short-listing there is bound to be more scope for subjective, arbitrary decisions.

During interviews, it is important that **all applicants are required to demonstrate their awareness of EO issues and, where appropriate, their understanding of the needs of students from ethnic minority communities.** Ideally these should be listed as essential criteria for all new teaching posts. Desirable criteria might include the potential candidates' ability to speak a local community language or to contribute positively to the school's EO/AR agenda.

43

■ 7.2 Appointing and retaining ethnic minority staff

If black and ethnic minority staff are conspicuous by their absence or confined to part-time, temporary or non-managerial roles, you are giving a very clear (albeit unwitting) message to parents and students that whatever your policy may say, the school doesn't practice what it preaches.

Regardless of your school's ethnic profile, your staff recruitment policy should state that **the school is committed to encouraging black and ethnic minority appointments at all levels within the organisation.** The potential benefits are self-evident. In schools serving many different communities, a multi-ethnic staff group is an invaluable human resource, serving as a vital link with the local community via professional networks, social contacts and links with parents. If they are valued and have a voice, black/ethnic minority staff can also

- ✔ provide added insights into the cultural, social and political experiences of local communities

- ✔ encourage colleagues to listen and respond to particular concerns

- ✔ contribute important skills such as the ability to speak a community language

- ✔ provide black/ ethnic minority students with a sympathetic listener or advocate

- ✔ serve as mentors or role-models

The arguments are no less persuasive in schools where the population is predominantly 'white'. Appointing teachers from minority communities will help to counter prevailing stereotypes. Such teachers will also serve as vitally important role models, particularly for young people who are only used to white authority figures. They may also bring fresh perspectives and insights to the curriculum, thereby helping to counter euro-centrism and racist assumptions.

Despite these potential benefits, black and ethnic minority teachers remain under-represented in most schools, reflecting the current situation on most teacher training courses.[5] Heads often point out that when teaching vacancies are advertised, black and ethnic minority applicants do not apply. If this is true of your school, or if you are keen to increase the number of black and ethnic minority appointments, some of the strategies listed in the checklist on the following page will help you to explore what else might be done.

■ 7.3 MAKING A CASE FOR POSITIVE ACTION

Where colleagues need to be convinced of the case for taking positive action to recruit more black/ ethnic minority staff, try identifying how many black and ethnic minority staff you have in teaching, non-teaching, part-time, managerial and decision-making roles, and expressing these figures as a percentage.

Your case will be easily made if you compare your findings with one of more of the following:

❑ the percentage of ethnic minority students in your school

❑ the percentage of ethnic minorities in your local community

❑ the percentage of ethnic minorities nationally

5   A study by the CRE in 1986 found that students of Afro-Caribbean and Asian origin made up only 1 in 40 or 2.6% of all students on PGCE, final year B Ed and other degree courses leading to qualified teacher status. About a third of PGCE courses and over two-fifths of B Ed courses had no ethnic minority representation whatsoever (Ethnic Minority School Teachers, CRE, 1988). The situation has improved only marginally since.

■ 7.4 CHECKLIST: APPOINTING THE RIGHT STAFF

Use the following checklist to explore some of the strategies the school could adopt to attract more black/ethnic minority applicants and ensure that your existing staff has the skills and awareness to take your EO(AR) policy forward.

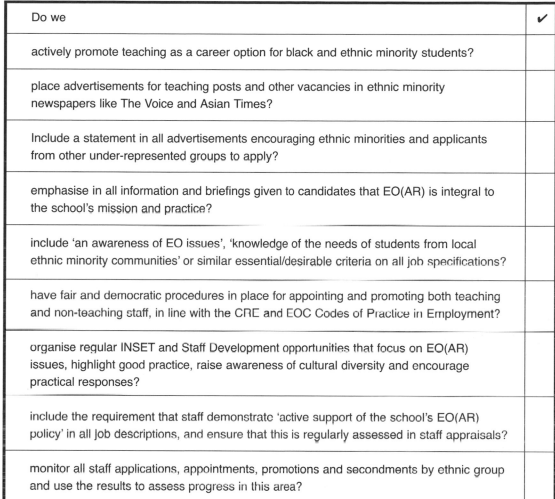

Do we	✔
actively promote teaching as a career option for black and ethnic minority students?	
place advertisements for teaching posts and other vacancies in ethnic minority newspapers like The Voice and Asian Times?	
Include a statement in all advertisements encouraging ethnic minorities and applicants from other under-represented groups to apply?	
emphasise in all information and briefings given to candidates that EO(AR) is integral to the school's mission and practice?	
include 'an awareness of EO issues', 'knowledge of the needs of students from local ethnic minority communities' or similar essential/desirable criteria on all job specifications?	
have fair and democratic procedures in place for appointing and promoting both teaching and non-teaching staff, in line with the CRE and EOC Codes of Practice in Employment?	
organise regular INSET and Staff Development opportunities that focus on EO(AR) issues, highlight good practice, raise awareness of cultural diversity and encourage practical responses?	
include the requirement that staff demonstrate 'active support of the school's EO(AR) policy' in all job descriptions, and ensure that this is regularly assessed in staff appraisals?	
monitor all staff applications, appointments, promotions and secondments by ethnic group and use the results to assess progress in this area?	

■ 7.5 Staff Development

INSET (in-service training) presents an ideal opportunity for staff to explore ways of developing and delivering aspects of your school's EO(AR) policy. As well as providing a forum for colleagues to consider the school's relationship with the communities it serves, a relevant programme of staff development that responds to identified or articulated training needs will ensure that **colleagues are regularly encouraged to discuss the EO(AR) issues that concern them and to work together to identify practical responses.**

Discussions about how to tackle racism and other forms of discrimination should not be restricted to INSET days, of course. **Staff meetings, working party discussions staff appraisals,** even **informal staffroom exchanges** can be instrumental in raising awareness of EO/AR issues. In schools where there is a culture of **sharing ideas and pooling resources**, discussing learning activities and approaches can be invaluable.

Mentoring and work-shadowing schemes that pair teachers who lack confidence or are keen to develop their skills in this area with colleagues who are more experienced or aware, can also be a highly effective way of supporting individuals, particularly where they are supported by **personal and professional development**, and **self-directed learning. Curriculum development activities** will also help to enhance individual skills. Most of the activities in this *Toolkit* are intended to be used flexibly in this way. Colleagues should be encouraged to try them out in a variety of settings, adapting the tasks to meet their specific requirements or contexts.

■ 7.6 Approaches to INSET

Staff concerns about other priorities could breed resistance if discussions about racism and diversity are given precedence over other EO issues or seen as unrelated to the day-to-day work of the school. In this context, devoting an entire INSET day to 'Antiracism' could be a recipe for disaster. Apart from the potentially emotive title ('*Why focus just on racism?*'), there may be legitimate concerns that other training needs are being over-looked. However, in schools where antiracism is seen as 'part of everything we do' or as one of a number of strategic responses that are regularly addressed on INSET days, **the inclusion of EO/AR activities in all staff training and of 'race and other equalities implications' on all agendas is seen as normal practice.**

Racism can be an emotive issue and the prospect of discussing it may leave colleagues feeling defensive or wary. For trainers and facilitators, this means giving extra careful thought to the title and aims of your programme or agenda item and to how discussions will be handled, particularly if people step outside the 'comfort zone' and strong emotions are expressed. The challenge to the chairperson or facilitator is to diffuse the situation without losing the learning opportunity it presents. This is equally true of the one-to-one discussions that take place between colleagues in the staffroom, in meetings or during staff appraisals. Again, if **EO/AR considerations are integral to staff and manager appraisal, departmental discussions and the developmental work of the school,** there is more likely to be an open and positive climate when staff address or debate EO/AR issues.

■ 7.7 DISCUSSING RACISM: A CHECKLIST for FACILITATORS

Whatever its theme, the most successful INSET relies on explicit ground-rules, clear aims and skilled facilitation. The checklist below suggests some of the steps facilitators can take to ensure that **staff discussions about racism are safe, comfortable and properly managed.** Use it when planning staff development sessions, working through the activities in the Toolkit, or chairing meetings where institutional racism or related issues are on the agenda.

KEEPING IT SAFE...
- ✔ Suggest or negotiate ground-rules to help create a safe, comfortable environment
- ✔ Explain the aims or desired outcomes of the session and what you hope to achieve in the time available
- ✔ Explain how the session will be structured and how long activities or inputs are likely to take
- ✔ If the time allows, include an 'ice-breaker' to get people thinking and communicating
- ✔ Make sure everyone has a chance to share their views and experiences, regardless of their position in the school hierarchy or how shy or confident they are
- ✔ Encourage respect for the fact the others may have different views and experiences
- ✔ Encourage colleagues to be frank and to respect confidentiality
- ✔ Ensure that the group makes good use of the time available and doesn't stray from the task or agenda item
- ✔ Always invite colleagues to evaluate the session and acknowledge what they have learnt or achieved

MANAGING CONFLICT
- ✔ Try to stay in control
- ✔ Listen carefully to what's being said
- ✔ Avoid taking sides
- ✔ Give people time to calm down
- ✔ Remind them of relevant ground-rules
- ✔ Invite others to contribute their views so that the issues don't become personalised
- ✔ If criticisms are aired, focus on attitudes – not individuals
- ✔ Be ready to return to the underlying issues at a later date if they need further discussion

46

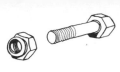

■ 7.8 Developing your INSET agenda: an example

Bridge End School INSET:
POLICY DEVELOPMENT DAY
10th January 2000 (9.30-3.30)

OVERALL AIM
❑ to develop a framework for drafting and implementing a revised Antiracist/Equal Opportunities policy for the school

OBJECTIVES
❑ to explore some of the key Equal Opportunities issues in school with particular reference to 'race' and gender issues
❑ to explore what constitutes good practice by looking at how Equal Opportunities/ Antiracism is delivered in other schools in line with OFSTED's current inspection criteria
❑ to agree the key areas that need to be included in the policy
❑ to consider some of the practical implications involved in developing and implementing it

OUTCOMES
By the end of today, we should all have had a chance to
❑ share our understanding of racism, sexism and other forms of discrimination
❑ consider what constitutes good Equal Opportunities practice in schools, with reference to OFSTED's inspection criteria
❑ discuss and agree the essential elements to be included in the school's revised Equal Opportunities policy
❑ explore some of the practical implications involved in developing and implementing the revised policy
❑ prioritise areas for action or further development
❑ agree a school-wide action plan

UNIT 8: Equality Assurance

> **OUTCOMES**
>
> Completing this unit will help to ensure that
>
> ✔ the school is committed to a rolling programme of consultation and self-scrutiny that leads to continuous improvement
>
> ✔ staff are prepared to ask appropriate questions and to examine the effects of their practices and procedures on a regular basis
>
> ✔ self-assessment activities give rise to explicit EO/AR objectives and targets against which staff can measure progress
>
> ✔ there is a consultative, 'bottom-up' approach that takes full account of the views and suggestions of individual staff and students and makes full use of established staff and student forums, working parties and school committees
>
> ✔ equality considerations are integral to the school's quality assurance process, which relies on both quantitative and qualitative evidence
>
> ✔ self-assessment activities derive from explicit EO/AR criteria and are approached with the same rigour that is applied to other statutory areas of provision.
>
> ✔ The Equality Assurance (EQA) process is overseen by an (E)Quality Review group that includes student, staff, parent, governor and community representation and qualitative evidence

Governors, teachers and headteachers are rightly concerned with providing and assuring quality and the highest possible standards of achievement. This necessarily …involves attention to issues of equality as well. Quality and equality strengthen and support each other, and neither is complete without the other.
Equality Assurance in Schools, Runnymede Trust, 1993

■ 8.1 What is Equality Assurance?

Equality Assurance or EQA involves integrating equality considerations into your school's quality assurance system. It works best if **the school is committed to a rolling programme of consultation and self-scrutiny that leads to continuous improvement**. The approach calls for close monitoring of the school's policies and provision in all key areas; regular consultation with staff, students, parents and community representatives; and the development of strategic responses to counteract bias, racial inequality and the effects of structural and institutional discrimination.

The HMI case suggests that, where **staff are prepared to ask appropriate questions and regularly to examine the effects of their practices and procedures**, there is less room for complacency and 'unwitting' institutional racism. Good practice indicators derived from commonly agreed standards that contain explicit or implicit EO/AR criteria can help schools to 'measure' progress and evaluate their achievements in a rigorous and systematic way, especially if staff are required to produce objective evidence of perceived strengths.[6] This approach ensures that EO/AR considerations are central to your quality assurance process and are 'mainstreamed' rather than 'bolted on'. It also encourages a

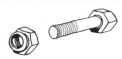

proactive response to evidence of discriminatory practices or procedures and other identified weaknesses.

Equality assurance has proven most effective in organisations where **self-assessment activities give rise to explicit EO/AR objectives and targets against which staff can measure their progress** (see Unit 4, Action Planning – a strategic approach). These should complement the strategic objectives in your school's three-year development plan. They should also reflect the commitments made to students and parents in your EO/AR policy. In other words, they should arise naturally from the life and work of your school.

Where they are not already in place, standard procedures for monitoring, reviewing and refining the school's targets and objectives on a regular (annual) basis will need to be agreed. Ideally, managers should ensure that **there is a consultative, 'bottom-up' approach that takes full account of the views and suggestions of individual staff and students and makes full use of established staff and student forums, working parties and school committees.**

■ 8.2 Who should drive the Equality Review process?

It helps if **the EQA process is overseen by an (E)Quality Review group that includes student, staff, parent, governor and community representation.** As well as ensuring that EQA procedures are fair and representative, the existence of the group will help to ensure that **Equality Assurance relies on explicit EO/AR criteria and is approached with the same rigour that is applied to other statutory areas of provision.**

With the support and endorsement of senior managers, your (E)Quality Review Group can play an important role in helping to combat people's doubts about the process by establishing innovative mechanisms for soliciting their views, suggestions and criticisms. One of its key responsibilities is therefore to make sure that consultation mechanisms are dynamic and rely on a variety of strategies such as the use of suggestion boxes, playground surveys, random checks, interactive feedback in tutorials, school web-sites and similar methods.

■ 8.3 Gathering qualitative evidence

Racism is too complex and entrenched for easy solutions, and there are many who would question the validity of an NVQ-like approach. Consultation and self-assessment activities for quality assurance purposes may appear mechanical or time-consuming, and there are likely to be doubts about the value of these exercises in schools where monitoring and equality assurance activities are seen as mere box-ticking or number-crunching.

Those involved will need to be persuaded that they are engaged in a meaningful dialogue with managers and decision-makers, particularly those who control the purse strings. They will also want regular feedback supported by evidence that any weaknesses or suggested improvements have been properly considered, and the resource implications explored. Otherwise the school's declared commitment to quality and continuous improvement could seem empty and rhetorical.

You may find you need to 'sell' equality assurance to students, too. Like staff, they will take surveys, suggestion boxes and other evaluation exercises seriously only if they can see what happens to their comments and criticisms – and if they feel safe enough to make them. This means ensuring that pupil surveys and questionnaires are anonymous, easy to complete and state clearly how people's views and suggestions will be used.

■ 8.4 STUDENT SURVEYS: GETTING AT THE ANSWERS YOU WANT

Student surveys and questionnaires need careful thought if they are to solicit meaningful responses. Stating an opinion or making a criticism can feel risky, especially if the teacher asking the questions is someone they don't trust. Ticking boxes will seem pointless, unless you believe your views will be valued. When consulting students about their experiences of equality and discrimination in the school, you will need to take these feelings into consideration and work at getting them to take the exercise seriously.

For example, how are you to

✔ explain the purpose of the survey or questionnaire?

✔ ensure confidentiality and anonymity?

✔ develop simple, statements that students will understand and relate to?

✔ devise a simple and efficient way of grading or categorising their responses?

✔ monitor and analyse their responses by ethnic group, year group gender and other relevant categories?

✔ use their views and criticisms to actively inform the school's ethos, practices and policies?

✔ give students feedback on how their views have made a difference?

Use this as a checklist to help you **develop a questionnaire or similar resource**, the purpose of which is to elicit students' feelings about their experience of discrimination and equality in the school. You may also want to develop a similar resource to use with staff or parents.

■ 8.5 EQUALITY ASSURANCE: A STRATEGIC FRAMEWORK

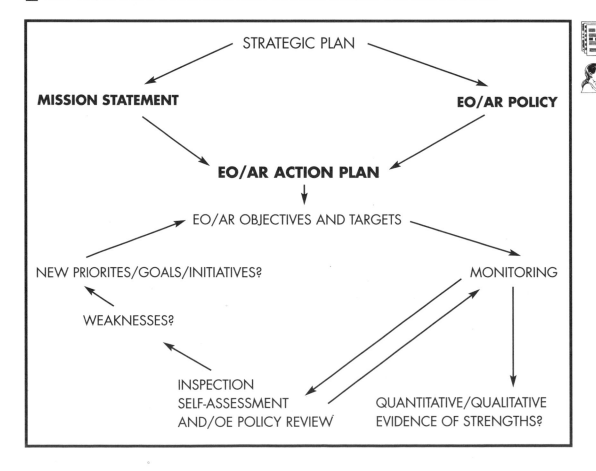

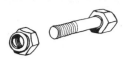

■ 8.6 EQUALITY ASSURANCE: DEVELOPING YOUR APPROACH

People are more likely to engage with an activity if they have an overview of the process and can identify a clear role for themselves within it. Use the strategic framework outlined here to review or develop your school's approach to (E)quality assurance and to identify specific roles and functions for individual staff and identified groups of students.

Self-assessment: a practical example

The example below shows how self-assessment at school-wide and departmental levels give rise to continuous improvement. When discussing it, bear in mind that although the necessary form-filling or report-writing may be the responsibility of one individual, identifying the strengths and weaknesses and agreeing overall grades should be the end result of a consultative exercise involving a representative cross-section of the school community.

Good practice indicators	yes/ no?	evidence of strengths?	evidence of weaknesses?	grade 1-5?	action needed?
The school conveys a consistent message that diversity is celebrated and racism is outlawed.	Yes	• *Mission/policy statements* • *Regular use of reception/ common areas to display students work* • *Use of community language in signs/communication with parents* • *Annual EO event* • *Multi-ethnic staff group* • *Positive feedback from parents*	• *No-procedure in place for identifying and removing graffiti* • *Record of name-calling incidents shows increase* • *Lack of positive Images of Travellers/*	2	• *Agree procedures w/school caretaker for recording/removing graffiti* • *'no to name-calling'* • *Develop a curriculum response* • *locate/order posters/learning resources* • *and organise some staff development*

Grade 1 = **outstanding** – many strengths and few weaknesses
Grade 2 = **good** – the strengths clearly outweigh the weaknesses
Grade 3 = **satisfactory** – strengths but also some weaknesses
Grade 4 = **less than satisfactory** – the weaknesses clearly outweigh the strengths
Grade 5 = **poor** – few strengths and many weaknesses

51

Note

6   In colleges, 'sector expectations' were established by the FEFC(Further Education Funding Council) in 1997, ensuring that the framework and criteria for equality assurance are explicit. They are used by the FEFC Inspectorate to verify the results of colleges' annual self-assessments and serve as a common standard that is applied throughout the sector. Schools, on the other hand, must rely on their interpretation of broad directives from OFSTED, the DfEE and LEAs when reviewing provision or preparing for inspection, leaving room for misinterpretation.

■ 8.7 GOOD PRACTICE INDICATORS: AN OVERVIEW FOR USE IN SELF-ASSESSMENT

The outcomes highlighted throughout this section can be used as good practice indicators when preparing for inspection or in self-assessment and (e)quality assurance exercises. Use the following pro forma for any one of these purposes. They will help you to assess in the eight areas listed.

1. MEETING LEGAL REQUIREMENTS

Good Practice Indicators	yes/no?	Evidence of strengths?	Evidence of weaknesses?	Grade 1-5?	Recommended action
✔ school governors understand the legal and statutory case for tackling racism and take a lead in this area					
✔ managers understand the need to use carefully targeted monitoring to scrutinise the school's performance in key areas					
✔ governors, managers and staff have considered all reasonably practicable steps to prevent discrimination					
✔ managers are able to convey the need for staff to respond actively to racism and empower staff to do so					
✔ grievance procedures are transparent, efficient and fair					
✔ managers understand the importance of logging and analysing complaints about racial discrimination from parents, students and employees					
✔ staff respond fairly and consistently to all racially-motivated incidents and keep a detailed record					
✔ staff receive clear, consistent guidance and regular staff development					

2 DEVELOPING YOUR POLICY

Good Practice Indicators	yes/no?	Evidence of strengths?	Evidence of weaknesses?	Grade 1-5?	Recommended action
The school's EO/AR policy					
✔ serves as a public declaration that the school takes racism and other forms of discrimination seriously					
✔ provides an explicit framework for whole-school change and development					
✔ is used as a consultation, planning and self-assessment tool and as a formal yardstick against which to assess progress					
✔ addresses discrimination in all its forms					
✔ actively informs the day-to-day life and work of the school					
✔ is seen as realistic and achievable by staff, parents and students					
✔ was developed and is actively supported by those who are expected to implement it					
✔ is easy to understand and appropriate for different audiences and uses					

3. TURNING POLICY INTO PRACTICE

Good Practice Indicators	yes/no?	Evidence of strengths?	Evidence of weaknesses?	Grade 1-5?	Recommended action
The school has					
✔ a school-wide working party or focus group leading a whole-school response					
✔ an explicit agenda and realistic aims					
✔ consultation, debate and regular two-way communication					
✔ the aims and desired outcomes of all consultation meetings and other policy-related discussions are explicit					
✔ the results of monitoring and any consultations, surveys or questionnaires are fed back in an interesting way					
✔ discussion of the policy is integrated into the school's existing planning, evaluation and review cycle					

4. ACTION PLANNING STRATEGIES

Good Practice Indicators	yes/no?	Evidence of strengths?	Evidence of weaknesses?	Grade 1-5?	Recommended action
When involved in **action planning**, staff seek to develop goals, targets and initiatives that are the end result of a process of consultation					
ensure that the goals and initiatives derived from your policy are PRECISE, ACHIEVABLE and TIMED					
distinguish between what is essential in the short term and what is desirable in the long term					
encourage whole-school ownership by involving all sections of the school community					
agree termly or annual review dates that complement existing priorities					
appreciate that qualitative feedback from students, parents and colleagues is just as important as numerical evidence of 'success'					

5. MONITORING FOR CHANGE

Good Practice Indicators	yes/no?	Evidence of strengths?	Evidence of weaknesses?	Grade 1-5?	Recommended action
Ethnic monitoring is actively used to					
✔ develop an accurate social and ethnic profile of your school					
✔ serve as a reference point when evaluating outcomes and achievements					
✔ provide evidence of new or changing circumstances, statistical trends and patterns					
✔ give some insights into the unwitting effects of institutional racism					
✔ the areas and categories used for monitoring purposes are relevant to departmental needs					
✔ the interpretation of any quantitative data is verified, using qualitative methods					
✔ you take full account of other considerations like students' gender, entitlement to free school meals and individual learning needs.					

6. IMPROVING YOUR SCHOOL ENVIRONMENT

Good Practice Indicators	yes/no?	Evidence of strengths?	Evidence of weaknesses?	Grade 1-5?	Recommended action
✓ the school conveys the message that diversity is celebrated and racism is outlawed					
✓ young people learn in an environment that prepares them to live in a multi-ethnic society					
✓ there is no offensive graffiti					
✓ posters, art and displays of students' work featuring non-European themes are displayed in common areas					
✓ a Code of Conduct that promotes respect for one another and the environment is prominently displayed in classrooms, staffrooms and other common areas					
✓ the school has a proactive response to antisocial behaviour that seeks to reduce conflict and promote interpersonal skills					
✓ staff and students are at ease discussing diversity and antiracism, when issues arise					
✓ These changes are part of an on-going, strategic, school-wide response					
✓ governors, managers and others responsible for the recruitment and selection of staff are trained to take full account of EO(AR) considerations					

7. STAFFING AND HUMAN RESOURCES

Good Practice Indicators	yes/no?	Evidence of strengths?	Evidence of weaknesses?	grade 1-5?	Recommended action
✔ governors, managers and others responsible for the recruitment and selection of staff are trained to take full account of EO(AR) considerations					
✔ all applicants are required to demonstrate their awareness of EO issues and, where appropriate, their understanding of the needs of students from ethnic minority communities					
✔ those involved in shortlisting or interviewing candidates understand the importance of adhering to fair, objective selection criteria					
✔ the school is committed to encouraging black and ethnic minority appointments at all levels					
✔ staff are regularly encouraged to discuss the EO(AR) issues that concern them and to work together to identify practical classroom responses.					
✔ the inclusion on all training agendas of specific activities on 'race and other equalities implications' is seen as normal practice					
✔ staff discussions about racism are comfortable and properly managed					

8. EQUALITY ASSURANCE

Good Practice Indicators	yes/no?	Evidence of strengths?	Evidence of weaknesses?	Grade 1-5?	Recommended action
✔ the school is committed to a rolling programme of self-assessment leading to continuous improvement					
✔ teachers are prepared to ask appropriate questions and to scrutinise the effects of their practices and procedures on a regular basis					
✔ self-assessment activities have given rise to a strategic plan that includes explicit EO/AR targets against which staff can measure their progress					
✔ self-assessment activities give rise to explicit EO/AR objectives and targets against which staff can measure their progress					
✔ there is a 'bottom-up' approach that takes full account of the views and suggestions of individual staff and students, established staff and student forums,working parties and school committees.					

WHAT'S IN PART TWO?

1. PLANNING OUTCOMES

2. HOW EACH UNIT IS STRUCTURED

3. OVERVIEW OF UNITS AND TEACHING OUTCOMES

4. TEACHING ABOUT RACISM: SOME GUIDELINES

5. CHECKLIST: HOW CONFIDENT AM I?

6. APPROACHES TO TACKLING RACISM

7. EVALUATION ACTIVITIES

TEACHING UNITS:

UNIT 1: *HISTORY*
Activity1: What is Racism?
Activity 2: Life Maps
Activity 3: Slavery and the Slave Trade
Activity 4: Colonialism
Activity 5: Memories
Activity 6: Consequences

UNIT 2: *STEREOTYPES*
Activity1: What are Stereotypes?
Activity 2: How do Stereotypes work?
Activity 3: Never judge a book by its cover...
Activity 4: Stereotypes and soap operas
Activity 5: Stereotypes that sell
Activity 6: Same story, different paper...

UNIT 3: *ATTITUDES*
Activity1: Ebony and Ivory?
Activity 2: The same-race adoption debate
Activity 3: Living separate lives
Activity 4: Labels
Activity 5: Exploring identity
Activity 6: Celebrating our differences

UNIT 4: *VIOLENCE*
Activity1: Sticks and Stones
Activity 2: 'Victims' under attack
Activity 3: Ethnic Cleansing
Activity 4: Media responses
Activity 5: Lessons from the Lawrence Campaign
Activity 6: Combatting racial violence

UNIT 5: *RESPONSES*
Activity1: Challenging racism
Activity 2: Messages from the far right
Activity 3: Homebeats
Activity 4: Music with attitude
Activity 5: Changing the rules
Activity 6: Campaigning for change

PART TWO

HAMMERS AND TONGS

'with great effort or energy'
(Collins Concise Dictionary)

This section suggests some approaches and learning activities that you can use to address racism and related topics in the classroom. How much effort and energy is actually required of you will depend on your context, teaching skills and prior knowledge, as well as your experience of the issues. But if you follow the advice on planning and preparation, the units and individual exercises should help you in your endeavours. The activities will encourage students to

❑ explore the historical roots of racism and how racist ideas and stereotypes have evolved

❑ understand the need to challenge racism in school as well as at home and on the streets

❑ appreciate the benefits of having a positive sense of cultural identity

❑ accept personal responsibility for their own attitudes and behaviour towards others

The exercises and discussion topics will complement Key Stages 3 and 4 of the National Curriculum, although some may also be suitable for use with younger children. Use them as part of a planned tutorial or PSE curriculum with explicit EO/AR objectives. Or select one-off exercises or activities that will reinforce the group's prior learning or complement messages you want to convey in your own subject area.

The suggested activities should also give you ideas for assemblies, and can be adapted for use in after-school clubs and other less formal learning contexts.

1. PLANNING OUTCOMES

By working through these introductory notes before planning which activities to use, you will get an overview of what each unit contains, and gain insight into the different approaches you could adopt and their relative merits and drawbacks. You will also appreciate why it is important that you and other **classroom teachers engaged in planning and preparation make every effort to...**

✔ **create a learning environment that is 'safe' and encourages students to share their thoughts, feelings and concerns**

✔ **develop clear aims, common ground-rules and a shared understanding of key words**

✔ **use whatever is happening in the world to raise awareness and encourage on-going discussion, debate and self-reflection**

✔ **respect and take account of students' individual identities and experiences, their differences and similarities, their social attitudes and religious affiliations**

✔ **avoid making stereotypical assumptions about what it means to be ''white''**

✔ **take account of individual identities and experiences, as well as changing social/ religious attitudes**

✔ **use the books and resources listed to assist your own learning**

✔ **take part in relevant staff or curriculum development activities**

✔ **create an ethos of relative safety and a readiness to listen and empathise with others' views and experiences**

✔ **evaluate whether the selected exercises and learning approaches have succeeded in influencing students' views**

2. HOW EACH UNIT IS STRUCTURED

TEACHING OUTCOMES

Use these to help you...

✔ with lesson or curriculum planning

✔ when introducing individual units or activities

✔ when developing or summarising teaching outcomes

PROMPTS

Use these to...

✔ explore specific issues

✔ help structure classroom discussions

✔ prepare the group for follow-up activities

DISCUSSION TOPICS

Use these when...

✔ expanding or structuring discussions in class

✔ identifying topics for assignments or project work

✔ preparing materials and back-up resources

✔ encouraging awareness and critical thinking

✔ exploring ideas for further research, homework or class assignments

CLASSROOM ACTIVITIES

Use the suggested activities (or develop your own) to...

✔ consolidate what has been learnt

✔ give you further ideas for project work, coursework, homework or one-off assignments

✔ inform lesson and curriculum planning

CHECKLIST: THINGS TO DO

Use these lists when thinking about resources you will need on the day and to point you to the books and other learning resources you could refer to when preparing different topics or developing handouts. The titles listed will also help you to explore themes and topics in greater depth and expand your knowledge of this area.

3. OVERVIEW OF UNITS AND TEACHING OUTCOMES

Use this list of essential and desirable TEACHING OUTCOMES to help you select the Unit(s) you need to work through. They should help you to pinpoint particular attitudes or themes and locate the most suitable activities for your group.

Teaching Units	Teaching outcomes: Essential	Desirable
1. HISTORY	By completing the selected activities, students will have...	By completing the remaining activities, students will also gain...
	• an understanding of the historical and psychological causes of racism • awareness of the connection between the Slave Trade, Britain's imperial past and today's multicultural society	• knowledge of contribution made by people from the Asia, Africa and the Caribbean to the 1st and 2nd World Wars and to Britain's post-war economic revival
2. STEREOTYPING	• an appreciation of how racial stereo-typing underpins racism • awareness of the role the mass media can play in perpetuating or challenging racist stereotypes	• a more detailed understanding of the function of some stereotypes and how crude generalisations help some people to 'make sense' of their world • knowledge of some common stereotypes of black people and of the historical and contemporary contribution they have made to society
3. ATTITUDES	• a critical awareness of popular attitudes towards 'race', difference and multiculturalism • clearer views and more positive feelings about personal and cultural identity	• appreciation the effect other people's attitudes can have on our thoughts, behaviour and/or feelings • some insight into contemporary social attitudes towards trans-racial adoptions and relationships
4. VIOLENCE	• an understanding of the causes and effects of racial violence • an awareness of some of the steps that can be taken to combat it	• awareness of the media's role in reporting racial violence • knowledge of the events that led to the Stephen Lawrence inquiry and the Macpherson Report
5. RESPONSES	• An appreciation of how effective people can be when they challenge or confront racists • an appreciation of how different forms of cultural expression (music, dance, drama etc.) can help to construct, challenge or change social attitudes	• insight into the strategies and key messages of racist and antiracist organisations

4. TEACHING ABOUT RACISM: SOME GUIDELINES

■ 4.1 CREATING SAFETY

However consistent your messages, they will be competing with the attitudes of friends and family members as well as the powerful views and stereotypes your students hear expressed in the media every day. Young people's views about racism, culture and personal identity are still developing. Like girls or young people with physical disabilities, black young people are constantly exposed to negative messages about what they can be and do. If you are to work with these views and stereotypes, they first have to be aired. You will need to think hard about how to **create a learning environment that is 'safe' and encourages students to share their thoughts, feelings and concerns.**

■ 4.2 SELECTING ACTIVITIES

The activities you select will be influenced by a number of factors such as the students' age, the requirements of your subject area and the length and number of sessions available. Ideally, you should opt to **work through one or more of the units as way of raising general awareness** in tutorials or as part of a PSE course. However, if the group has addressed some of the issues before – or is exploring them elsewhere on the curriculum – it will make more sense to select one-off activities, allowing you to reinforce prior learning or encourage students to look at things from a new perspective. Whatever your approach, be aware of the dangers of overkill.

Some of the units and activities can be adapted to meet the subject requirements of the National Curriculum at key stages 3 or 4. The level at which this work is pitched and the nature of classroom activities will be determined by the demands of the subject, but teachers of Humanities, Art, English, Drama, History, Sociology, Media Studies and Citizenship Education should have no difficulty finding suitable activities to include. Activities that use statistics or ICT (Information and Communications Technology) could also be adapted for use in Maths or ICT classes. When thinking about how to incorporate the activities into your particular subject, bear in mind that the prompts and classroom activities are only suggestions. They may need to be reworded or reworked to support specific learning needs or teaching outcomes. Students will benefit most if you do this kind of thinking in advance. Whatever your subject, the activities will work best if you **develop clear aims, common ground-rules and a shared understanding of key words** (see page 89).

■ 4.3 KEEPING IT REAL

Racism is a dynamic issue, meaning that the cultural, social and political context and the language we use to discuss it are constantly evolving. Your students' interests and learning needs will reflect the realities, priorities and controversies of the day. Whether you overhear them talking about last night's episode of *Eastenders*, the murder of a rap artist or the latest ethnic cleansing atrocity, **use whatever is happening in the world to raise awareness and encourage on-going discussion, debate and self-reflection.** There will always be local incidents, human interest stories, interesting statistics, information on the Internet, news events or national debates in which racism, 'race' relations and other related issues are a prominent feature. Exploit them!

■ 4.4 HANDLING FEELINGS

People's feelings about racism, difference and personal identity are rarely easy to explore, particularly in a classroom setting. You may have to break through a wall of embarrassment, feigned boredom or defensiveness before you can get the class to engage. Once you do, it is important to **avoid making stereotypical assumptions about what it means to be 'white' or 'black'.** You may well unearth some crude racist views, especially in predominantly 'white' schools, but you are equally likely to uncover sensitive and positive attitudes towards difference. It is not uncommon for white young people to have black friends, step-parents or married relatives. Some may prove to be of dual or mixed heritage themselves or to have parents or grandparents who originally came to Britain as immigrants. Others may have strong feelings about racism because of personal experiences of being bullied, taunted or excluded because of their appearance or special needs.

Even if such differences are not immediately apparent to you, there will be others arising from their social class, gender or home circumstances that you can draw on. These and other differences will probably prove to be your most valuable teaching resource.

■ 4.5 RESPECTING DIFFERENCE

In multi-ethnic classrooms, where young people are often grappling with conflicting experiences of school, home, and youth culture, there are likely to be some strong and sometimes contradictory feelings about religious, linguistic, cultural or personal identity. By giving students the space to define who they are and how they see themselves, you convey an important message that you value their experience. This also helps to break down barriers by revealing what they have in common. Your ability to demonstrate that you **respect and take account of students' individual identities, their differences and similarities, their social attitudes and religious affiliations** will ultimately determine the credibility of your key messages.

To make the best use of these activities, you will want to feel confident and sufficiently prepared to handle the questions and differing viewpoints that may emerge. You are most likely to achieve this if you **use the books and resources listed in Part Three to assist your own learning** and seize every opportunity to take part in relevant staff or curriculum development activities. Keep an eye on the news for relevant items and make a case for papers like the *Voice* or *Asian Times* to be ordered for the staffroom. If teaching about racism is new or unfamiliar territory, this will help you to develop suitable language and some confidence. It will also expose you to a wide range of different views that you can draw from.

■ 4.6 CREATING OWNERSHIP

Once in the classroom, you can encourage 'ownership' of the ideas and activities by involving students in planning and preparation and demonstrating that, within reason, you will try to respond to whatever they raise. Having clear ground-rules will help you to manage discussions by helping to **create an ethos of relative safety and a readiness to listen and empathise with the views and experiences of others**, however unfamiliar they may be. Having explicit teaching outcomes will help you to judge what is immediately relevant. If questions arise that you are unprepared for, be ready to admit that you don't have all the answers. This is a valid response whether you are black (and therefore 'expected' to know them) or white (and possibly expected not to). If necessary, give yourself time to think things through – or invite the group to seek out the answers by doing their own research or talking to friends and family members. This will give you some space as well as encouraging group ownership of the issues.

■ 4.7 CREATING A SUPPORTIVE CONTEXT

Your work in the classroom will be most effective if it is part of a whole-school strategy to convey a consistent message that antiracism, with its attendant values of respect for diversity and fair treatment for all, is 'part of everything we do'. This message will have credibility only if young people are able to see the evidence with their own eyes, reflected in the life and work of the school. Clear policies, explicit codes of conduct, effective grievance procedures and consistent staff responses will create the right context for this work by reinforcing the message that racism is undesirable and will be actively opposed (see Part One). Good quality staff training and effective communication will also be central to your efforts, and will help to develop your confidence.

For some, this scenario may seem like a far-off utopia. You may lack the support of your Headteacher or Head of department or find yourself working on these issues in relative isolation. You may have to seek out ways to create a supportive context for doing this work. It helps to identify someone to talk to who understands your context and supports what you are trying to do, preferably a fellow teacher. If you can't find an appropriate ally among your colleagues, try to access networks of like-minded teachers in neighbouring schools. Remember that once you've done the necessary groundwork, when you close your classroom door you can move mountains...

■ 5 CHECKLIST: HOW CONFIDENT AM I?

Racism is not an easy subject and you may find that you shy away from it in the classroom because you aren't confident that you can handle what it brings up in you or in the young people you are working with. Use the following checklist to help you prepare.

✔ How confident am I to broach this topic and the messages I want to get across? Do I need to read up on or discuss anything with someone first?

✔ Is racism/cultural identity something most of this group will feel comfortable discussing? If not, what reactions do I anticipate?

✔ Are there likely to be some individuals who resist or strongly identify with particular messages? Do I know why?

✔ How much preparatory work will I need to do with this group – for example, agreeing boundaries or defining key terms?

✔ How can I ensure that the discussion feels 'safe'? What ground-rules could I suggest – for example, about coping with angry feelings or being ready to learn from conflicting viewpoints?

✔ Have I thought through the discussion prompts and how I will deal with the responses they could provoke?

✔ How will I deal with any conflict or resistance? If certain students 'act up' or express offensive views, can I 'keep the equality' by challenging the ideas rather than the individual concerned?

✔ Am I clear what I'm aiming for and how I will achieve it? Have I defined the particular skills or competences and the changes in awareness, attitude or behaviour that I am hoping for?

✔ Do I have everything I need? Are there any handouts to prepare, videos to order or back-up resources to be located in advance?

✔ Which classroom activities are most suited to the needs of this group? How will I evaluate the extent to which individual attitudes have been challenged, expanded or changed?

If any of your responses suggest you are not yet fully prepared, make a list of what else you will need to do and try to set yourself some achievable deadlines.

■ 6 APPROACHES TO TACKLING RACISM
AN OVERVIEW

There are many different ways of tackling this issue. All have potential advantages, drawbacks and resource implications. Before you do any detailed planning, you may find it useful to spend some time discussing or thinking about the different approaches you could adopt and which are most suited to your own working context. For example:

Look at the first column. Tick the approaches that are most likely to meet your group's particular needs and spend some time thinking about what they will entail. You will find this easier if you...

work down the lists of potential advantages and drawbacks, ticking the ones that are most likely to apply in your working context. This should help you to think about what could be done in advance to promote the advantages or avoid some of the drawbacks you anticipate

look at the 'delivered via...' column, and tick anything on this list that you (or your school) would find hard to deliver

look at the 'requires...' column and tick anything your school already delivers. Then go back and reflect on what it could deliver – for example, by providing staff development, reallocating existing resources or establishing new procedures. Turn these into specific objectives or targets (see Part 1, Unit 4: Action Planning Strategies).

You will probably find that no single approach is adequate in itself and that it is best to aim for a healthy balance. The range of activities and learning approaches you choose should reflect this.

APPROACHES TO TACKLING RACISM

Approaches	Advantages	Drawbacks	Delivered via	Requires...
Institutional: developing a whole-school policy and school-wide strategies to address institutional racism in its various forms, including the curriculum, staff training etc.	gives staff, parents and students a clear message that the school takes this issue seriously and is committed to change provides staff and governors with a shared vision and a strategic framework for tackling institutional practices and procedures that may be discriminatory or fail to take account of legal/statutory requirements.	may assume that written declarations of intent are sufficient in themselves to bring about change if developed without consultation and regular review of policy outcomes, may be seen as irrelevant or unrealistic could prove ineffective or divisive unless there is staff/student 'ownership' and an understanding of the benefits to all	a well-publicised policy statement linked to the school's overall mission and a school-wide implementation strategy to accept managing/co-ordination/ consultative forums in which staff, students, parents and other relevant parties can help to formulate or review policy outcomes on-going staff induction and development to raise awareness of the policy and related procedures; and to develop resources/good practice guidelines	credible, realistic, timed outcomes named individuals who are willing monitoring/evaluating responsibilities a designated budget for INSET, curriculum development and other essential activities efficient monitoring and review procedures
Informative: teaching students the historical/ socio-economic 'facts' about slavery, colonialism, immigration, racial disadvantage, asylum seekers etc.	provides an historical and political basis for understanding and exploring complex issues can be used to explore links with other equalities issues such as class, gender, nationalism, global citizenship etc. and to encourage identification with other groups.	may assume that racism results from irrationality or ignorance may underestimate the power of institutional and ideological racism and the influence of parents, the media, peers etc. may put white students on the defensive or make black students angry, resulting in polarisation	Planned lessons/ units/ courses tasks/assignments/guest speakers films/videos theatre workshops input from and into the community e.g. local antiracist campaigns, racial violence/harassment units etc.	curriculum strategy access to suitable curriculum resources and time to research/order/ trial/ develop them a designated budget for speakers, books, films, posters, video hire, travel, other essential resources internal or external expertise
Experiential: encouraging identification with what it's like to be the victim of discrimination or social injustice	encourages personal identification with what it feels like to be excluded, harassed, ridiculed, etc heightens awareness of the effects of racist/ other unacceptable behaviour	relies on its emotional appeal may trivialise racism by defining it as isolated/individual acts or reducing it to concerns about personal injury	formal/informal workshops involving discussion and/or role-play structured games/activities	appropriate room and atmosphere for games and workshop activites staff who feel confident to handle strong emotional/difficult group dynamics

Approaches	Advantages	Drawbacks	Delivered via	Requires
Multicultural: organising classroom activities/ visits/ cultural events and/or exchanges to increase understanding and appreciation of other cultures	encourages intercultural contact and an appreciation of the benefits of cultural diversity provides an opportunity to 'sample' or experience aspects of other cultures/ religions may increase students' understanding of and ability to value their own or other cultures can encourage positive feelings of cultural identity	may imply that cultural differences rather than racism are 'the problem' may assume that the dominant culture is the norm to which others should conform or be compared can encourage a 'zoo mentality' by emphasising the exotic or curious may reinforce existing prejudices based on stereotypical representations of other cultures/religions/ lifestyles may overlook questions of economic/ ideological power and social hierarchy which are central to understanding racism	visits/exchanges/attending festivals/ school trips abroad etc. events or curriculum-based activities involving cookery, music, dance, world religions, traditional dress etc input into the community via voluntary work, pupil involvement in multicultural projects etc contacts with parents and community groups	adequate funds for outings/activities cultural events pupil/parental/community involvement a multicultural staff group or access to community organisations that can offer advice and information staff training to encourage respect for/awareness of different cultures, religions and issues of cultural diversity
Moralistic: appealing to students' sense of decency or personal morality	provides a 'moral yardstick' with which to understand/ challenge racism may have a positive influence on attitudes/behaviour in other areas both in and outside the school – e.g. bullying	effective in the short term but can leave historical and political roots of racism unchallenged may assume (Christian) values that are not shared by all students	challenging/ highlighting personal/ social injustices formal/informal religious or moral instruction input from/ into the community via fund-raising activities and/or support for global/ ecological/ humanitarian campaigns	an explicit Code of Conduct liaison with religious/humanitarian organisations morally persuasive staff

Approaches	Advantages	Drawbacks	Delivered via ...	Requires
Attitudinal: providing counselling for individual students or racism awareness training for staff	can encourage greater self-awareness	may be too personalised or psychologically orientated, resulting in anger, defensiveness or 'guilt tripping' may emphasise personal responsibility at the expense of political/school-wide responses and strategies may ignore issues of institutional power	structured discussion with groups/ individuals appropriate group activities, including role-play/ assertiveness workshops etc	in-house counselling expertise or input from an external trainer staff with training in basic counselling skills who feel confident to handle strong emotions/difficult group dynamics
Targeted provision: providing self/ cultural/ historical awareness-raising or exclusive groups **Targeted language classes:** providing ESOL and/or Community Language classes for identified groups of black/ ethnic minority students	provides a 'safe' forum for exploring shared experience of blackness, racism exclusion, harassment, displacement, etc promotes assertiveness and positive feelings of cultural/social identity encourages full participation by otherwise under represented or isolated groups improves communication and/or language skills	may assume one shared experience and overlook important religious/cultural/ linguistic diversities may encourage assumptions about preferential treatment thus risking further isolation/harassment of members of the targeted group may be perceived as second class or 'ghetto' provision or as a response to a deficiency	formal/ informal group discussions use of talks/films/videos/plays exhibitions to examine relevant cultural and social issues music/cookery/other shared cultural activities that encourage group identity EAL/community language provision	community consulation, outreach and/or home-school liaison guidance or input from parents, community respresentatives etc. access to suitable resources staff with the skills, expertise and confidence to deliver
Punitive: automatic punishment of racist attitudes or behaviour	gives everyone a clear message that racism will not be tolerated counteracts feelings of helplessness in the target or victim of racist abuse	results in the punishment of overtly racist individuals rather than their enlightenment relies on sanctions or force and may encourage alienation or polarise loyalties suppresses overt racist activity but fails to challenge the ideology or individual views	direct personal intervention accompanied by enforceable sanctions including fixed term or permanent exclusion adherence to an explicit, well-publicised Code of Conduct and realistic, enforceable sanctions staff training to develop challenging, conflict-resolution or assertion skills	a well-publicised Code of Conduct clear, enforceable sanctions confident, assertive staff

■ 7. EVALUATION ACTIVITIES

It is always good classroom practice to **evaluate whether your key messages have been positively received** and your teaching outcomes achieved. Where racism is concerned this is not always easy to do. Students may tell you what you want to hear, reluctant to reveal their true opinions for fear of being judged or condemned. You may also find that your successes in the classroom are relatively short-lived and that the views of peers or family members ultimately hold more sway. It could take several years before the messages you are trying to convey fully sink in. Despite these drawbacks, you can still use evaluation to **ascertain whether there have been any** short-term changes in attitude and to judge the relevance of **particular units, activities or learning approaches.**

WHAT HAVE I LEARNT?

Develop your own questions or use the ones suggested below to encourage the class to think about what they have learnt:

WHAT HAVE I LEARNT?

Think back over the discussions we've had today/ this week/ this term. What have you learnt? List the three most important messages

....

....

....

Were there any you messages or views you strongly agreed or disagreed with?

Have any of your views changed as a result? If so, which ones?

Do you feel more confident now to challenge racist views or behaviour?

Can you complete the following sentences in your own words?

Britain is a multicultural society because..

....

Racism is..

Stereotypes are...

The best response to racist attitudes or behaviour is to...

....

When I think about racism, I feel...

....

SAYING WHAT WE MEAN

Make a list of some of the key terms you are planning to introduce in your next session and invite each individual in the group to jot down in advance what the term means to them. Make it clear that there are no 'wrong' answers at this stage, only different views and opinions. Once they have completed the exercise or classroom activity, get them to return to their original definitions and consider whether they would want to amend them in any way – and if so, how. Their responses will hopefully provide some evidence of improved understanding – not just of the words, but of the issues they refer to.

WHAT WE LIKED BEST

Get members of the group to discuss *what they liked best* and *what they liked least* about the unit or activity and to *explain why*. Log their responses so that you can analyse them and give some feedback. If there's time, invite them to suggest how they would have structured and delivered the unit and try to incorporate some of their suggestions next time.

BODY SCULPTURES

Working in groups of three or more, invite them to think up a 'body sculpture' using their arms, legs, posture, facial expressions, chairs and other available props to convey all the different feelings they have about the topic you have been discussing. Allow time for students to explore their emotions before they begin and to rehearse. Each group then constructs its sculpture, holding the pose for a few minutes before inviting the others to tell them what feelings they were attempting to convey.

ART GALLERY

Working on their own or in pairs, get the group to talk in some depth about their responses to the unit or the lesson and its messages. Then ask them to draw or paint the feelings or reactions they have described. Display their work on the walls of the classroom, as if it were an art gallery, and invite the group to browse for five minutes. Then spend some time discussing together what each picture is trying to convey (preferably without any help from the person concerned) and whether it reflects their own feelings about racism.

FILM MAKERS

Working in small groups, invite the class to consider what issues they would want to cover if they were asked to make a short film about racism. Ask them to list their ideas and, if time allows, suggest that they produce

- ❑ an outline of the stories and key messages they would include in the film

- ❑ a script or storyboard for one of the scenes or

- ❑ a dramatised extract

Whichever they choose to produce, it will give you some insight into how well they have understood the different messages and whether any previously-held views have been challenged.

UNIT 1: HISTORY

PROMPTS

- ❑ Racism has a long history. Britain is a multicultural society because of slavery, colonialism and other historical events
- ❑ If we are to understand why racism is still a problem today, we must understand something of that history
- ❑ People are usually racist because they are afraid or insecure about physical and cultural differences, which they perceive to be important
- ❑ Racial differences are perceived or socially constructed – underneath 'the paintwork' we are all the same

TEACHING OUTCOMES

Essential:

- ❑ an understanding of the historical and psychological causes of racism
- ❑ awareness of the connection between the slave trade, Britain's imperial past and today's multicultural society

Desirable:

- ❑ knowledge of the contribution made by people from the Asia, Africa and the Caribbean to World Wars One and Two and to Britain's post-war economic revival

PROMPTS

- ❑ What do you understand by the term 'racism'? Can you describe what the word means to you?
- ❑ Have you ever experienced or witnessed racism of any kind? If so, what happened? And how did it make you feel?
- ❑ Why do some people hold racist views? What do they stand to gain?
- ❑ Why is Britain a multicultural society? Is it just an 'accident of history'?
- ❑ Why were people from the Caribbean, Africa and the Indian sub-continent ready to uproot themselves and come to Britain in the years after the war?
- ❑ What are the advantages and disadvantages of living in a multicultural community or society? Can you list some of them?
- ❑ Do any members of your family hold strong views about racism? How much have your own views have been influenced by theirs?

DISCUSSION TOPICS

- ❑ The historical reasons for today's multicultural communities, including Britain's involvement in the slave trade and the rise and fall of the British empire
- ❑ Pseudo-scientific theories about 'race', racial 'types' and characteristics and how these have developed since the 19th century
- ❑ The psychological reasons for racism and why fear, insecurity, ignorance or racial envy can cause some people to hate
- ❑ Historical examples of where racism can lead such as the slave trade, the Holocaust, apartheid etc.
- ❑ The contribution made by the black servicemen and women and 'the colonies' to World War Two
- ❑ Post-war migration and how immigrant workers helped to 're-build the Mother Country'
- ❑ The reasons why people can become refugees or migrants
- ❑ Experiences of being an immigrant or refugee in Britain today
- ❑ The advantages and disadvantages of living in a multicultural world, society, community or 'global village'

HISTORY: CLASSROOM ACTIVITIES

Activity 1: What is racism?	Activity 2: Life Maps	Activity 3: Slavery and the slave trade
Ask the group to compile a list of **all the words and ideas that come to mind when they hear the term 'RACISM'.** This can be a done as a word-storm. Then, working in small groups, get them to think of **specific examples or illustrations** of one or more of the different terms on their list – for example, prejudice, ignorance, treating someone differently – ideally from their own experience. After discussing them, each group should choose the example that illustrates the term best. Use their feedback to establish how well they understand the key terms you will be using. If appropriate, reproduce p.89-94 as a handout and use it as a basis for agreeing working definitions. You could follow this up by watching a relevant video. For example, 'VISUAL REALITIES (Camden Race Equality Council, 1999) explores young people's views about racism; or get hold of WHITE LIES (Swingbridge Video). Both videos will encourage them to think about racism in greater depth.	Working in groups of 4 or 5, ask each to study a large map of the world. Give each person a handful of stickers or pins. If possible, everybody in the group should be given their own colour. Ask them to place their pins or stickers on the countries they have a connection with because of: ❑ Family ties ❑ Travel or migration ❑ Somebody they know ❑ The clothes they are wearing today ❑ The food they have eaten over the past week Each person then has 2 or 3 minutes to explain the reasons for choosing the countries they have. You can select any or all of the above, but bear in mind that the outcome of the discussion that follows will be determined by the choice you make. For example... ❑ Family ties will show how common it is for people to marry outside their own culture and how misguided it is to believe in notions of racial purity ❑ Ties due to travel or migration will show how common it is for people to move around the world or to have relatives or connections in other countries ❑ Ties due to something they've eaten or are wearing will show how dependent we are on global trade and the cheap labour of people in poorer countries	Use an appropriate stimulus to get the class to think about what it meant to be a slave. This could be... ❑ an image of the chains and other devices used for restraint ❑ an extract from a slave narrative or a novel about slavery ❑ an episode from 'Roots' or 'Amistad' or one of the documentaries about slavery from Channel 4's 'Untold' series (etc.) Use the discussion this provokes to explore the reasons for the slave trade and what it was like to be captured, enslaved and put to work on the plantations. Supplement the discussion with suitable reference materials. Then select one of these activities to be done individually or with one or two others: ❑ write a diary entry describing a day in the life of a fictitious slave before capture, during the Middle Passage, and as a fieldworker on a plantation ❑ Compose a letter to the Governor of Jamaica arguing the case for abolishing slavery ❑ Write a newspaper article describing the capture and punishment of a slave who attempted to escape
CHECKLIST: THINGS TO DO ✔ Reproduce definitions of key terms (p.89-94) ✔ Gen up on any definitions you're not sure about (see: *Dictionary of race and ethnic relations*, E.Ellis Cashmore, Routledge (latest edition)	✔ Locate world map – Peters' projection (The Festival Shop, Birmingham see Useful Addresses p.101)	✔ Locate a suitable resource (e.g. visual image, extract from a novel, video etc.) to stimulate the initial discussion (see p.98 Books and resources/HISTORY for ideas)

75

Activity 4: Life under colonialism	Activity 5: Memories	Activity 6: Consequences
Look at an extract from a film or a book about life in the colonies, preferably one made in the 30s, 40s or 50s. Use it to get a discussion going about what it might have felt like to be colonised or what life would be like if Britain was invaded and subjected to colonial rule by a far-away country If possible, suggest they do some research – for example... ❏ Find a map of the world that depicts the former British Empire and Protected Territories and try to find out how many people and countries were affected ❏ choose a former British colony and find out what you can about how that country got its independence and the extent of any bloodshed or conflict involved ❏ access the relevant sections of the HOMEBEATS CD-rom or find a book in the library that describes how the colonies were originally acquired; write a summary of your findings	Ask them to talk to their grandparents or other elderly people they know about their memories of life before, during or immediately after the 2nd world war. Alternatively, ask them to find out how black, Jewish, Irish, German and/or Japanese people were seen at the time Where possible, get them to record their interviews on cassette so that they can be heard and discussed by everyone else. Even better, invite one of the interviewees to come in and talk to the group about their memories Use the discussion that follows to ❏ consider how language and attitudes have changed over the past 50 years ❏ explore the debt owed to black people for their efforts during the war and their contribution to Britain's subsequent economic prosperity ❏ refute arguments that unemployment, housing shortages and poverty are the fault of 'immigrants' or 'all the refugees'. There are also a number of films and documentaries that explore these subjects in greater depth which you could use as a stimulus or follow-up to these discussions	Use a relevant newspaper extract or TV documentary depicting some of the horrors of genocide or 'ethnic cleansing' to provoke discussion about racism, nationalism, antisemitism and xenophobia and where they can lead if they go unchallenged. Alternatively, make contact with a local refugee organisation and ask them if any of their members would be willing to come in and talk about their personal experiences of becoming a refugee or asylum seeker. If so, make sure that the speaker is given clear instructions and understands your aims. Use these stimuli to get the group to consider how fear or 'race' hatred can result in human rights abuses, displacement and genocide. If possible, get them to do some research of their own. The websites of organisations like AMNESTY INTERNATIONAL are an excellent source of information.
CHECKLIST: THINGS TO DO ✔ Locate a world map (preferably one showing the British empire circa 1950 – ask your librarian) ✔ Order HOMEBEATS (from the Institute of Race Relations – see p.98-101) ✔ Find an extract from a relevant film or book about life in the colonies ñ films like Sanders of the River, Zulu etc are ideal – see *BFI Black Films Catalogue* (address on p.100).	✔ Locate interviewing equipment (ideally tape recorders or a video camera) ✔ Gen up by reading some first person accounts (see p.101-102 for bookshops that can supply you with an up to date list of what's available) – and reproduce these as handouts ✔ Find out if any reminiscence work is being done with black elders in your area – they may well have photographs, a video or a speaker for you. Your local branch of Age Concern should be able to help	✔ Contact your local Council or Voluntary Action forum for a list of refugee organisations and/or the names of individual refugees ✔ Locate campaign reports, newspaper cuttings or a TV documentary depicting ethnic cleansing or genocide

KEY MESSAGES
- ❏ People tend to justify racist views by stereotyping others and blaming them for society's problems
- ❏ Stereotypes can undermine our sense of who we are by suggesting that how we look or speak determines how we act
- ❏ TV programmes, advertisements and popular newspapers perpetuate stereotypes by misrepresenting or under-representing different groups

TEACHING OUTCOMES
Essential:
- ❏ an appreciation of how racial stereotyping underpins racism
- ❏ awareness of the role the mass media can play in perpetuating or challenging racist stereotypes
- ❏ knowledge of some common stereotypes of black people and of the historical and contemporary contribution they have made to society

Desirable:
- ❏ a more detailed understanding of the function of some stereotypes and how crude generalisations help some people to 'make sense' of their world

PROMPTS
- ❏ Can you give an example of a 'stereotype'? What are they and why do you think people need them?
- ❏ Can you describe any TV programmes you've seen that portray ...
  Black people as muggers or criminals?
  Asian people as unable to talk proper English?
  Jewish people as tight-fisted or mean?
  Irish people as terrorists or drunkards ?
- ❏ Can you think of examples of similar stereotypes you've come across in a popular newspaper, magazine or comic?
- ❏ What are the most common media stereotypes of the (ethnic/ social) groups you belong to? And what arguments would you use to disprove them?
- ❏ Have you ever had to question your own, your parents' or your friends' stereotypical views? Who or what made you want to do that?
- ❏ Can programmes that make fun of racist views help to challenge people's racism? (What films or TV programmes have you seen that do this well?)
- ❏ Do you know of anyone whose views have changed because of something they saw on TV?
- ❏ Can you name any black people, past or present, who have contributed to... politics? the media? medicine? science? sport? the music industry? Which lists are the longest and why do you think this is so?
- ❏ Can you describe any TV or billboard ads you've seen lately that portray black people in a positive or non-stereotypical way? Are things changing?

DISCUSSION TOPICS
- ❏ The socio-economic function of stereotypes and how they help to maintain the balance of power in society
- ❏ 'Brawn not brain': the historical reasons why black (African) achievements are usually only acknowledged in the fields of sport and entertainment
- ❏ The representation, misrepresentation and under-representation of black people in the media
- ❏ How the media portrays famous and infamous black people
- ❏ Contemporary and historical examples of individual black people who have contributed to science, medicine, technology, the arts etc.
- ❏ How the media influences public opinion and helps form social attitudes about different ethnic, national or social groups
- ❏ How soap operas, documentaries and other TV programmes can encourage healthy public debate and help raise awareness of controversial issues
- ❏ Controversial advertising campaigns that rely on or debunk popular stereotypes – e.g. the Benetton ads, the CRE poster campaign
- ❏ A survey of who has power, influence and control in the mass media
- ❏ A survey of the accents, dress codes or social attitudes that are considered most acceptable to 'mainstream' audiences

STEREOTYPES: CLASSROOM ACTIVITIES

Activity 1: **What are stereotypes?**	**Activity 2:** **How do stereotypes work?**	**Activity 3:** **Never judge a book by its cover...**
After agreeing a working definition of the term 'stereotype', ask the class to identify some of the popular stereotypes of one or more of the following groups: ❑ Japanese or American tourists ❑ British football fans abroad ❑ teachers and teenagers ❑ women and men ❑ lawyers and social workers ❑ English, Irish, Scottish or Welsh people ❑ people with disabilities ❑ rich people and people who are on income support Then work with them to draw up a list of the most common stereotypes of refugees, black youth. Single mothers and other groups of black people. If you are concerned about inviting them to do this, get them to work alone or in pairs, giving them a limited time to list their stereotypes and come up with as many counter-arguments as they can think of Your aim is to show that, while most stereotypes may be based on a kernel of truth, they are usually unfair or unfounded and there are always going to be exceptions to the rule	Use an appropriate visual aid – for example one of the CRE's recent antiracist poster campaigns – as a basis for discussing the function of stereotypes and their role in maintaining the status quo. (Their 1998 campaign was controversial because it relied on popular racial stereotypes to promote more public awareness of what black people in Britain have achieved.) Alternatively, you could use one of the more controversial Benetton ads, or some very stereotypical images of black people in sport, entertainment, menial labour etc as a stimulus Get the class to design and produce a poster or poster campaign of their own. Their images should use or debunk common stereotypes to present a positive message. They can do this individually, in pairs, in small groups or as a class project Make the posters into an exhibition for display, preferably in the foyer, canteen or another common area where others will be able to see and discuss it You may want to follow this activity up by watching THE EYE OF THE STORM (Concorde Video and Film Council) which is the film of a classroom experiment showing the effects discrimination on young children. Although not specifically about stereotyping, it shows graphically how the acting out of prejudice can damage children's self-esteem and create conflict in a school setting.	Contact families or speak to someone from Age Concern or a local community group with the aim of identifying some local individuals who have unusual or atypical occupations. Invite them to come in and speak about their work and how they came to be doing it. If you want to encourage ownership of the event, get members of the group to make the call or compose the letters of invitation. Make sure that the speakers are properly briefed and that they understand that the purpose of their input is to challenge popular stereotypes and provide young people with some alternatives. Before the speakers introduce themselves, ask the group to try and guess as much as they can about each person – for example, their name, who they are, what kind of family they have, where and how they live and what jobs they do. Keep a record of what they say. Once the speakers have finished talking about themselves and their work, invite the class to return to their original ideas and suggestions. The object is to consider how accurate they were and whether their perceptions were based on stereotypes or genuine observations.
CHECKLIST: THINGS TO DO ✔ Gen up on racial stereotypes in advance. There is a useful section on this in the HOMEBEATS CD-rom – or see Books and Resources on p.95-101 for more ideas	✔ Order a set of CRE posters/ postcards from the Commission for Racial Equality) or locate other suitable visual material ✔ Locate coloured felts/ A3 paper for posters ✔ Order THE EYE OF THE STORM to watch in class	✔ Make contact with Age Concern or another relevant voluntary organisation to identify local people with unusual or atypical occupations as possible speakers

78

Activity 4: Stereotypes and soap operas 😊	Activity 5: Stereotypes that sell	Activity 6 Same story, different paper...
Record a relevant episode from one of the popular soap operas in which black characters or race-related issues (e.g. mixed relationships, racial abuse etc.) are prominent, and watch it together. While watching, ask the group to think about... ❑ how 'typically' the black characters behave ❑ how well the script-writers have tackled the (race-related) issue ❑ how else the characters might have behaved ❑ whether the characters come across as stereotypes or real people? ❑ whether the episode will help to raise public awareness or to challenge popular stereotypes You can follow this up by getting them to divide into smaller groups and re-write part of the script in a way that achieves this. If time allows, get them to role-play it or to present their ideas to the class It may also be worth getting hold of a copy of BLACK and WHITE IN COLOUR (BBC Enterprises) in which black actors like Lenny Henry and Judith Jacobs talk about the TV roles they've played and how they have dealt with media stereotyping	Get the group to go through some old magazines and newspapers and cut out and display as many advertisements as they can find that feature black people or depict non-Western cultures Ask them to study one or more of the ads in their display and explore the following questions, working in small groups: ❑ Why do you think the people who produced this ad decided to use black people or a foreign culture to convey their message? ❑ What message(s) are they trying to convey? ❑ What audience are they appealing to? ❑ Would this advertisement 'work' if the black person or people in it were white? ❑ What stereotype(s) or cultural assumptions are the advertisers relying on? When they have finished thinking about these issues, their task is to work together to design an alternative ad that uses black people or non-Western cultures without relying on racial or cultural stereotypes. Make an exhibition of their work and display it in a common area where others will also be able to see and discuss it	Ask the group to collect headlines and articles from as many different newspapers as they can find, covering the same (race-related) incident or concern. Alternatively, if you have access to the internet, get them to access the web pages of a selection of daily newspapers and download them Distribute these and, working in small groups, give them the task of highlighting the words and phrases that are most likely to influence or 'shape' the reader's opinion in the report they've been given. Get them to list these words/phrases on large sheet of paper Display their lists on the wall next to the articles concerned, so that the differences can be easily spotted and compared. Use the discussion that follows to address the following questions: ❑ What are the most obvious differences in the way each newspaper has reported this incident? ❑ Which words are most emotive? ambiguous? loaded? ❑ What is your idea of a 'typical' reader of (e.g.) the *Sun*? the *Telegraph*? the *Voice*? the *Asian Times*? Would you call your descriptions stereotypes?
CHECKLIST: THINGS TO DO ✔ Make/find a recording of a relevant episode from one of the popular soap operas (e.g. Eastenders, Brookside or Coronation Street) ✔ Order a copy of BLACK AND WHITE IN COLOUR (from BBC Enterprises, see page 100)	✔ Bring in a pile of old magazines, newspapers, journals and/or (travel/ sports/food) posters that are likely to contain images or advertisements featuring black people or a range of different cultures	✔ Locate a set of articles from a cross-section of different newspapers covering the same (race-related) incident or concern — on micro-film in your local library, or try downloading articles from their websites

79

UNIT 3: ATTITUDES

KEY MESSAGES
- ❑ When people take a stand against racism in their lives or their relationships with others, they can face considerable peer pressure
- ❑ A positive sense of your own identity is important if you want to resist this kind of pressure or challenge other people's assumptions

TEACHING OUTCOMES
Essential:
- ❑ a critical awareness of popular attitudes towards 'mixed race' relationships
- ❑ some strategies for questioning racist attitudes and challenging individuals who behave in a racist way
- ❑ clearer views and more positive feelings about personal identity

Desirable:
- ❑ appreciating the effect other people's attitudes about 'race' can have on our thoughts, behaviour and/or feelings
- ❑ insight into contemporary social attitudes towards trans-racial adoptions and relationships
- ❑ awareness of the competing cultural messages that help to shape our sense of identity

PROMPTS
- ❑ Countries like Britain and America are becoming increasingly multicultural, and 'mixed' marriages are growing. Why is this happening? And would you say it's a good or a bad thing?
- ❑ What arguments have you heard put forward by people who blame refugees, 'foreigners' or 'blacks' for the poor state of the NHS? the shortage of houses? high unemployment rates? street crime?
- ❑ What other attitudes would you define as racist? Do you have any examples from your own experience?
- ❑ Have you ever challenged someone about attitudes like these? If so, what did you say and how did they respond?
- ❑ Why is it sometimes harder to challenge the attitudes of a friend, a teacher or someone in your immediate family than, say, those of a total stranger?
- ❑ Some people justify racist attitudes by saying they are simply 'looking out for their own kind'. Do you think it's a good thing for people to look out for their own kind? Or to have a positive sense of their own personal, national or cultural identity?
- ❑ How would you identify yourself? Are you proud of your identity or are there bits you'd like to change?

DISCUSSION TOPICS
- ❑ The influence of peers/ family members on individual behaviour, attitudes and social identity
- ❑ The advantages and disadvantages of 'mixed' relationships
- ❑ The incidence of 'mixed' relationships in Britain and the effects this could have on social attitudes/behaviour
- ❑ The effect of apartheid laws in South Africa that kept the races apart and banned inter-racial sex
- ❑ The arguments for and against 'same-race' fostering and adoption
- ❑ Strategies for challenging racist comments and attitudes

ATTITUDES: CLASSROOM ACTIVITIES

Activity 1: Ebony and ivory?	Activity 2: The same-race adoption debate	Activity 3: Living separated lives
Use statistics showing the increase in the number of 'mixed' marriages in Britain to launch a discussion about people's attitudes to such relationships. Alternatively, watch a relevant film or video – eg 'Secrets and Lies', 'Coffee-Coloured Children' (Albany Videos) that explores issues of mixed parentage and identity. Get the group to identify any people they know who are in 'mixed' relationships or married to someone from a different nationality or culture. Solicit their views about well-known couples like Lenny Henry and Dawn French or characters from contemporary soap-operas. Invite them to talk about how others see the couple and how well they handle these attitudes. If the couple has children, or if there are young people in the group who can speak from personal experience, explore how they cope with the differences between their parents and with other people's attitudes towards them. For example... ❑ How do they feel about terms like 'half-caste'? ❑ How did they learn about their dual/ multiple heritage? Do they identify with one more than the other? As a follow-up to this discussion, the group could... ❑ conduct a school-wide survey of attitudes towards 'mixed' couples ❑ interview family and friends ❑ prepare a report of their findings.	Distribute copies of newspaper articles and other documents that argue for or against same-race fostering and adoption. Ask the group to make a list of the key topics or arguments they find. Invite them, in small groups, to compare their lists. Their task is to prepare a briefing paper for someone like an MP or well-known commentator who has to appear in a TV interview or documentary and argue the case for or against same-race adoptions. If time allows, role-play the debate, using volunteers from each group to make up the panel of speakers. As a preparatory or follow-up research activity, invite them to contact Social Services or their local Race Equality Council to find out how many children of mixed parentage are currently in care in the area. They may want to interview a local social worker or foster carer to explore the reasons why the percentage is often so high.	Get the group to think about the effects of the segregation laws in the USA or the apartheid laws in former South Africa that kept the races apart and banned inter-racial sex. Tell them to imagine that a law like this was passed in Britain and how it would affect people's lives. If possible, show them a relevant video – for example, a documentary about life under apartheid – and use this to stimulate a small group discussion in which they are asked to make a list of... ❑ the pros and cons of inter-racial marriage ❑ the arguments for and against racial segregation ❑ the advantages and disadvantages of being of mixed parentage Use these lists to stage a debate, in which opposing teams argue in support of the conflicting views. Have two teams put forward the different arguments, and conduct a vote at the end to determine whose arguments were most persuasive.
CHECKLIST: THINGS TO DO ✔ Locate statistics showing the incidence of 'mixed race' relationships in Britain (available from the Stationery Office – or see *Race in Britain Today* by Richard Skillington)	✔ Locate copies of articles and other documents giving the arguments for and against 'same-race' fostering and adoption – Social Work organisations will be able to help; also see the relevant sections of the 1989 Children Act	✔ Order or locate a relevant film or video – for example, Secrets and Lies or relevant a documentary about life under apartheid (see Concord Video and Film Catalogue or RESOURCES for ideas – p.100)

81

Activity 4: Labels	Activity 5: Exploring identity	Activity 6: Celebrating our differences
Introduce the group to a discussion about identity by inviting them to make a list of all the words that describe who they are or how they see themselves – for example, teenager, cockney, black British, Muslim, football fan etc. You could also watch Being 'White', (Albany Videos) which explores the issue of white identity	As a follow-up to the presentations in Activity 4, divide into small groups to explore the following questions:	Divide into two groups and invite them to wordstorm and log all responses to the questions 'what is culture?' and 'what is identity?' Post up the two lists and help them to tease out any differences and similarities.
Working in small groups of 3 or 4, their task is to 'unpack' the labels (e.g. 'what do they mean to you? To your parents? Friends? other people?) and then to select three or four 'labels' they all have in common	❑ What do we have in common as a group? ❑ What are our main differences? ❑ Do these differences matter? (why/why not?) ❑ Does the way we see ourselves affect how other people see us? ❑ Who or what gives us our sense of identity? ❑ Is our identity something we inherit, or is it something we can choose? ❑ How important is the influence of our family? religion? our peers? the media? ❑ Why is our identity or 'knowing who we are' important to most people? ❑ Does marrying someone from another national/ethnic group necessarily mean giving up your own identity? Or the identity of your children?	You can do this by handing out some definitions (from the dictionary or other relevant source) and using them for comparison. The discussion should draw out the many ways our cultures (i.e. what we do to celebrate/ make sense of life) and identities (i.e. our sense of who we are) can be influenced or transformed in a multicultural society. It should also lead them to think about any benefits or drawbacks.
They can feed these back verbally or, better still, give them 15 minutes to produce a drawing, dramatic scene or 'body sculpture' (see evaluation activities) that represents the labels they have chosen. The role of the rest of the group is to guess which labels they are illustrating and discuss whether they agree with the selection.		As a follow-up, get each person to fold a large sheet of paper into three and do a self-portrait in the central column. On one side, list all the activities, attitudes, artefacts etc. that represent their CULTURE; on the other side, make a list of everything that represents their IDENTITY. Display their work and get them working in pairs to explore what they like/dislike about themselves or, if it feels safer, what is unique and what they have in common with others.
	Use their feedback to consolidate the message that to be able to rise above other people's racist attitudes and assumptions, a positive sense of your own identity is vital.	
	You could follow up this activity by watching a relevant video – for example, Young, British and Muslim, Concorde Video and Film Council (address p.100), which explores the experience of young Muslims growing up in this country.	
CHECKLIST: THINGS TO DO ✔ Prepare the seating in a circle or semi-circle to encourage interaction and discussion ✔ Paper and felt tips, if needed	✔ Prepare the seating in a circle or semi-circle to encourage interaction and discussion	✔ Locate some definitions of the terms 'culture' and 'identity' in the dictionary or another relevant source ✔ reproduce the definitions as a handout

82

KEY MESSAGES

❏ Racism can lead some people to commit acts of violence or abuse or to join racist organisations

❏ The consequences of racial violence can be severe – for both the victims and the perpetrators

❏ Not all targets are victims – some people respond to racial violence and injustice by becoming antiracists

TEACHING OUTCOMES

Essential:

❏ an understanding of the causes and effects of racial violence

❏ an awareness of some of the steps that can be taken to combat it

Desirable:

❏ insight into how the media have responded to racial violence

❏ knowledge of the events that led to the Stephen Lawrence inquiry and the Macpherson Report

PROMPTS

❏ Have you ever been called names, shouted at, chased or beaten up? How did it make you feel?

❏ What kind of people commits racial attacks? What do you think makes them do it?

❏ The statistics show that the majority of racist attacks are by young people under the age of 30. Why do you think this is so?

❏ Should people found guilty of racially motivated acts of violence be given harsher sentences? Why?

❏ Who should be responsible for protecting people from racist attacks – the police or community vigilante groups?

❏ Which is best   to confront racists physically? to challenge their ideas? or both?

❏ Why are words like 'wog', 'nigger', 'paki' and 'paddy' considered by most people to be terms of abuse?

❏ Is it okay for black people to call each other 'nigger' or for Asian people to call each other 'paki'? Can you explain why or why not?

DISCUSSION TOPICS

❏ Statistical data showing the incidence of racial violence in the UK over recent years

❏ Examples from the press of the human consequences of racial violence – for example, Stephen Lawrence or Quddus Ali – and how it can ruin lives

❏ Police, media and community responses to Stephen Lawrence's murder; the Lawrence family's campaign to bring his killers to justice; and the recommendations from the Macpherson inquiry

❏ An investigation of how the media responded when Stephen Lawrence was murdered and how this compares with coverage of Richard Everett's murder by a gang of Asian youths

❏ Ways of challenging racist views and behaviour – either as an individual or in a group

❏ What to do if you want to report a racially-motivated incident or attack to a teacher or the police

❏ The origin, meaning and use of racist terms like 'nigger', 'paki', 'wog' etc. and how terms of (racial) abuse are used to debase and dehumanise others

❏ Contemporary or recent examples of 'ethnic cleansing' from Rwanda, Bosnia, East Timor, Kosova, Sierra Leone etc.

VIOLENCE: CLASSROOM ACTIVITIES

Activity 1: Sticks and stones...	Activity 2: 'Victims' under attack	Activity 3: Ethnic cleansing
Invite the group to 'word-storm' all the different terms of racial abuse they can think of – (for example, nigger, wog, paki, coolie, wop, chink, yid, kraut, frog, paddy, half-caste, etc.) Write these up boldly on a 'white' board or flipchart. (This kind of word-storm needs careful handling, but if you feel confident that you can manage their responses, you may want to extend the scope by inviting them to suggest terms that are used to abuse other groups – for example, gays, women or people with disabilities.) Ask if anyone has ever been called any of these names and spend some time talking about what it felt like. Then distribute the different terms to pairs or individuals and set them the task of researching their origins and meaning. This could be a homework assignment Get them to report back on their findings next time you meet, and use the discussion that follows to explore the following... ❑ Would you continue to use these terms now that you know their history and how hurtful they are? ❑ If someone black calls another black person 'nigger'; or if a gay group calls itself 'Queer Nation', does it help to 'take the power away' from the word, as some people claim?	Ask individuals who have witnessed, experienced or heard about acts of racial abuse or violence to describe how it felt or how they reacted. Alternatively, use a poem, newspaper report or extract from a novel that describes an act of racial violence Working in groups of 4 or 5, invite them to develop a role-play depicting one of the events or experiences they've looked at. Make sure that everyone has a chance to contribute ideas about when, where and why the abuse or attack took place, and what is said or done by the different people involved. The role-play should try to create sympathy either for the victim(s) or the perpetrator(s) After each group has acted out their role-play, get the class to discuss how it went. For example... ❑ how easy or hard it was to play the different roles ❑ how they would have responded if they had witnessed any of these incidents ❑ what the different parties involved could have done to diffuse the situation ❑ whether the perpetrators should be punished or re-educated – and if so, how?	Use an appropriate documentary or newspaper reports of 'ethnic cleansing' in Rwanda, Bosnia, East Timor, Kosova etc. to explore the extreme consequences of racism and xenophobia. Be sensitive to the distress that could be caused by eyewitness accounts of brutality, and make sure your de-briefing takes account of individual emotions Using the eyewitness accounts as a stimulus, give each member of the class time to write a poem, short story or essay about genocide or ethnic cleansing An alternative to individual poems is to write a class poem, with each person contributing one or two lines. Make sure the theme of the poem is clear to everyone and that the length of each person's contribution is specified Encourage them to perform it to others or prepare a presentation for another suitable occasion
CHECKLIST: THINGS TO DO: ✔ Find out what you can about some of the different terms of racial abuse and think carefully about how you will handle the word-storm	✔ Contact your local Race Equality Council or a similar organisation for information about what to do if you experience or witness a racial attack, and reproduce this information as a handout	✔ Locate an appropriate documentary or newspaper report depicting 'ethnic cleansing' in Rwanda, Bosnia, East Timor, Kosova etc

Activity 4: Media responses	Activity 5 Lessons from the Lawrence campaign	Activity 6 Combating racial violence
Use newspaper reports about the murders of Stephen Lawrence in Eltham in 1993 and Richard Everett in Somerstown, Camden in 1995 as a stimulus for comparing media responses to racial violence. Ask the class to suggest reasons why the media's response was so different and how else they think the press could have responded. If possible, invite a representative of the local Police, Racial Equality Council or a relevant campaign group to come in and speak to the group about... ❏ what they are doing to combat racial violence in the area ❏ what young people can do if they ever witness or experience an act of racial violence or abuse ❏ the steps that can be taken in school and in the community to prevent racist attacks and encourage positive community relations If you want to encourage ownership of the event, get the group to compose the letter of invitation	Use a relevant film, TV documentary or newspaper reports to explore the events which led to the Stephen Lawrence Inquiry. In particular, focus on the role played by Doreen and Neville Lawrence in drawing attention to their experiences at the hands of the police Use this discussion to explore the reasons for the Inquiry and the key findings of the Macpherson Report Working in small groups, invite the class to study the quotes by the different people involved and to make a list of the recommendations they would make to the police, schools and other social institutions responsible for challenging such views Then hand out copies of Macpherson's recommendations and ask them to compare their list with his. When reporting back, they should focus on... ❏ any of Macpherson's recommendations that they strongly agree with, and why ❏ any of Macpherson's recommendations that they strongly disagree with, and why Try to come up with a list of alternative recommendations that reflects the views of the whole class. If any of them could be applied to the school, get the class representative to put them forward to the appropriate committee	Give the group statistical information on the incidence of racial violence in the UK and ask them to say whether or why it surprises them Go on to discuss some of the things people could do to combat racial violence either as individuals, as a community or as a society – for example, writing to the press, taking part in a demonstration, campaigning for changes in the law etc. If possible, use examples of individual and collective action taken from the HOMEBEATS CD-rom or a particular organisation's campaign literature to inform this discussion and show that 'victims' can respond and take action Follow this up by getting students to work in small groups and develop ideas for a poster or advertising campaign that will highlight the damaging effects of racial violence on the community and encourage individuals to challenge and report racial incidents. Display this prominently in a common area of the school where others can see and discuss it Alternatively, they could develop a ten-point plan for reducing racially-motivated abuse or violence in the school and give it to their class representative for discussion at the next School Council meeting
CHECKLIST: THINGS TO DO ✔ Locate newspaper reports on the murders of Stephen Lawrence and Richard Everett (from libraries on micro-film or on the internet) ✔ Make contacts in the local Police, REC or a community group that supports victims of racially-motivated violence	✔ Locate a relevant film, TV documentary or newspaper reports about the events leading up to the Stephen Lawrence Inquiry ✔ Copy the key findings and recommendations from the Macpherson report and distribute as a handout	✔ locate statistical data showing the incidence of racial violence in the UK (available from HMSO – or see *Race in Britain Today* by Richard Skillington, Sage, latest edition)

UNIT 5: RESPONSES

KEY MESSAGES

- Groups and individuals who challenge racism can and do make a difference
- The music, fashion and cultural industries can play an important role in challenging racist views and assumptions by promoting positive messages and providing positive role models

TEACHING OUTCOMES

Essential:

- an awareness of how effective people can be when they challenge or confront racists
- an appreciation of how different forms of cultural expression (music, dance, drama etc.) can help to construct, challenge or change social attitudes

Desirable:

- insight into the strategies and key messages of racist and antiracist organisations

PROMPTS

- Do you know of any organisations locally that distribute racist literature or encourage racist behaviour? What tactics do they use to recruit people?
- Do you know of any local groups that have successfully campaigned against racism? How did they go about it?
- Can books, music, films, soap operas, plays etc. change a person's outlook? Do you know of any examples (e.g. novels, lyrics) that...
    - ...give a negative (racist, sexist, homophobic or similar anti-social) message?
    - ...give a positive antiracist message or raise people's awareness other important social issues?
- Do you think artists or groups become more popular when they convey positive social messages? Or does it put people off if they're 'too political'?
- Do you know of any artist or group whose lyrics have helped promote the interests of a particular group – for example, black people, women, gays, or people with disabilities?
- What can young people do to challenge racism in school, at home or in the local community? List some strategies
- What should teachers do to support those students who want to fight racism and other inequalities in school? List some strategies
- Do you think antiracism involves challenging people physically (through fights/ confrontations) or ideologically (through ideas/ viewpoints?)
- Apart from handing out leaflets or going on counter-demonstrations, what else can be done to prevent racist activity in the school or local community?

DISCUSSION TOPICS

- The messages and political aspirations of far-right organisations
- Antiracist organisations and why their activities are/ are not effective
- Common assumptions about who has access to housing, employment, health services etc.
- Musicians/artists/writers/playwrights etc. who address racism and other social issues through their music, writing, poetry or plays
- How artists/writers/musicians/poets etc. can act as our 'social conscience'
- The role of censorship and who controls the messages we are allowed to hear/ the images we are allowed to see
- The pros and cons of cultural fusion (e.g. in music, food, how we speak or dress)
- The importance of self-determination, self-organisation and self-awareness for social/ethnic groups that have experienced discrimination and marginalisation
- Practical antiracist strategies: what young people can do to help bring about change

RESPONSES: CLASSROOM ACTIVITIES

Activity 1: Challenging racism	Activity 2: Messages from the far right	Activity 3: Homebeats
Ask members of the group to list any comments they've heard or incidents they've seen where racism or cultural differences were a contributing factor	Using the messages and activities of a far-right organisation like BNP, get the group to think about what such organisations stand for and how they convey their racist propaganda (e.g. through graffiti, flyers, demonstrations, rallies, intimidation, racist attacks)	Using the HOMEBEATS CD-rom, get the class to explore how black communities in Britain have organised and campaigned against racist laws and practices over the past 30 years. Set them specific tasks – for example, to find out...
Distribute the comments and ask them to develop a role-play suggesting how the comment or behaviour could have been challenged		❑ the names of individuals who have made a difference
Once each role-play has been performed, summarise the different challenging strategies they have come up with and talk about which ones were most effective	If possible, get them to research some of this information themselves. They could start by developing a questionnaire to help them investigate the number, membership and influence of right-wing organisations locally. Use these to interview friends, family, neighbours, local shopkeepers etc. The library or the internet will also be a good place to look for such information. Invite them to feed back the results and discuss their findings	❑ how women have contributed ❑ how black people have helped to improve working conditions ❑ Invite them to report their findings to the rest of the group
As a follow-up activity, ask them to go back into their small groups and use what they have learnt from the role-plays to produce a 'checklist' for individuals who want to challenge racism at home, at school, at work or in the street		The aim is to get students to question the notion of 'passive victims' and to show how a relatively small group of people can bring about significant change
Post up their lists and tease out the strategies that are most likely to bring about changed attitudes or a positive outcome. Try to emphasise the importance of challenging the behaviour, not the individual	You may want to provide some statistical information that challenges popular racist assumptions about black people being a drain on housing, employment, health services etc.	Follow this up by showing them a relevant film or video – the BFI's Black Films catalogue (address p.100) will give you plenty of ideas.
CHECKLIST: THINGS TO DO ✔ Identify a suitable room and 'props' for use in the role-play	✔ Locate examples of the activities or philosophies of the BNP(British National Party), Combat 18, the Ku Klux Klan or a similar far-right (overtly racist) organisation ✔ Contact the Stationery Office for statistical data to counter assumptions that black people are a drain on housing, employment, health services etc.	✔ Order the HOMEBEATS CD-rom from the IRR (see p.101) ✔ Arrange for class access to a compatible computer and monitor ✔ Order a relevant film or video from the BFI Black Film catalogue (address p.100) and arrange for the class to watch it

87

Activity 4: Music with attitude	Activity 5: Changing the rules	Activity 6: Campaigning for change
Ask the group to select and bring in cassettes or music videos of one of the artists or groups they listen to whose lyrics... ❑ address issues like racial violence, discrimination, environmental issues or human rights ❑ promote racism, conflict, violence or other negative values or social attitudes Ask them to introduce their chosen artist or group and say why they like them or agree with the message(s) in their music. Invite others in the group to listen to, discuss and analyse each track. For example... ❑ Did they like the track/ agree with the person who introduced it? ❑ What message was the artist or group trying to get across? Did they succeed? ❑ Should musicians, writers and other cultural workers be our social conscience? Or is it better if they stay clear of controversial or political subjects? If possible, follow this up by playing the group some examples of songs that have a powerful antiracist message, and encourage them to write their own lyrics to a song that attempts to convey similar sentiments	Reproduce copies of the institution's EO/AR statement, Behaviour Policy or Code of Conduct and invite the group to identify what they like/ dislike about them. You may want to look at statements or policy extracts from other organisations, by way of comparison Go on to explore the reasons for such policies and statements, and whether they think written declarations can make a difference to how people behave at school or at work. If not, what else can schools and employers do to discourage racial harassment and discrimination? Make a list of their responses and explore any practical implications You may want to use this opportunity to invite the Headteacher or another senior colleague to come in and discuss the school's stance on racism and other EO issues and how it responds to racial incidents Working in small groups, get them to develop their own EO/AR statements or a Code of Conduct that could be used in school to discourage racism and other forms of antisocial behaviour. Alternatively, ask them to develop a questionnaire for use in a school survey about the effects/ effectiveness of the policy. They could present the results to the School Council for discussion/ adoption by the whole school	Find out about local groups involved in antiracist activities – for example, supporting victims of racial attacks, campaigning against the deportation of asylum-seekers, promoting more equitable world trade etc. Ask them to send you some literature or, if possible, to send someone along to talk to the class about their aims and activities and about how the group has mobilised support Work in small groups, to identify a similar concern either in school or the local community and to develop a plan of how they would go about setting up a campaign to tackle it. In particular... ❑ Who would they want involve? ❑ How would they get people's support? ❑ What messages would they want to convey? ❑ What changes would they want to bring about? If there's time, follow this up by getting them to develop some campaign literature – for example, a poster or a flyer – and make a display of their work to exhibit in a common area where others can see and discuss it
CHECKLIST: THINGS TO DO ✔ Locate a cassette or video player ✔ Find a recording of lyrics with a powerful antiracist/ social message – e.g., Bob Marley's 'War' or Labby Siffre's 'Something Inside so Strong' – the list is endless!	✔ Make copies of the school's EO/AR statement, Code of Conduct or extracts from another relevant document ✔ Locate similar policies/ codes from other organisations to use for comparison	✔ Make contact with local/ national campaign group(s) and ask for flyers, posters, articles, other campaign literature ✔ Invite someone from the group to come in and speak

PART THREE

BRICKS AND MORTAR

WORDS WE USE

If this is your first attempt to discuss or address antiracism in your school, or if you expect different or controversial views to be expressed, you will probably need to **invest time in developing a shared understanding of the meaning and use of key terms.** Words like 'racism' are loaded, and will undoubtedly suggest different things to different people. The use of certain terms – like 'black' or 'half-caste', for example – can be highly emotive. By agreeing working definitions of the key words you will be using to convey thoughts, feelings and ideas, you will avoid common misunderstandings and help people to communicate their views and ideas more effectively. The definitions suggested below are not 'written in tablets of stone'. Ideally, they should be used to generate discussion and, where time allows, to come to a shared understanding of key terms.

89

WORDS USED TO DESCRIBE INDIVIDUALS and GROUPS

Black

is commonly used to refer to those who, because of their 'race', colour or ethnic origin, are visibly or identifiably different from the ethnic majority. The term was first used positively in the 1960s when the rise of urban black consciousness in the USA, Britain and Africa popularised slogans like 'black is beautiful' and 'I'm black and proud'. Originally used to refer exclusively to people of African descent, it now serves as a 'catch-all' and may include people from a much wider range of cultural, social, linguistic or religious backgrounds. For example, as well as second generation Africans and African-Caribbeans, it may include Asians, people of dual heritage, as well as non-white refugees from countries like Vietnam or the Philippines.

When used in this generic way, BLACK refers to a shared social experience rather than a person's skin tone. Some people argue that such generalisations deny people's differences and ignore or undermine their national identity. The term nevertheless continues to be a convenient way of acknowledging people's shared experience of racism, with its common historical roots in slavery, colonialism and neo-colonial (economic) exploitation. Because of this, it is a 'political' term with which many non-white ethnic minorities still choose to identify.

Associations with evil, death or negativity in the English language has led to a number of everyday phrases in which the word BLACK is used not to describe colour (descriptively) but to suggest or imply something bad (metaphorically). People who are aware of the power of language will try to avoid phrases like 'it was a black day for Britain' or 'he was the black sheep of the family' and to question negative associations of blackness with anti-heroes like Darth Vader in Star Wars, the occult etc. However, it is not necessary, as some sections of the media have implied, to avoid using the term 'black' descriptively (e.g. black coffee, black board)

Coloured

was the 'polite' term used in the 40s, 50s and 60s to refer to non-whites. It was also used by black people as an alternative to the term 'negro' (for example, in the 1940s there were Coloured People's Associations in London, Cardiff and Edinburgh). Nowadays for a number of reasons it is not how most black people would choose to describe themselves. The use of the phrase 'two coloured lads' by one of the investigating officers during the Stephen Lawrence inquiry and his failure to recognise that the term was offensive, has been widely cited as evidence of the outdated attitudes that prevail in the police force.

Ethnicity

refers to a person's distinct sense of cultural and historical identity based on them belonging by birth (or in some cases by marriage) to a particular ethnic group. The term is often misused and the concept frequently misunderstood.

Ethnic Minority

or MINORITY ETHNIC are terms of convenience. Both are used to refer to people who are identifiably different to the ethnic majority because of their parents' or grandparents' origins. Sometimes these differences are barely apparent. Sometimes they are obvious because of language, accent, dress or religion.

The terms ETHNIC MINORITY or MINORITY ETHNIC are most commonly used to refer to...

- ❏ people who were born abroad and have settled in the Britain
- ❏ people who are British-born but whose parents or grandparents were born overseas
- ❏ people of Southern European, Eastern European or North African origin – for example, Turks, Cypriots, Kurds, Armenians, Greeks, Italians, Moroccans etc.
- ❏ religious and linguistic minority communities – for example Muslims, Jews, Travellers
- ❏ new arrivals (asylum-seekers and refugees) from places like Somalia, Eritrea, Bosnia or Kosova
- ❏ white minorities – for example Irish, Scottish and Welsh people

It is worth noting that in some inner-city areas, ethnic 'minorities' are increasingly likely to be the majority. In Greater London, for example, ethnic minorities make up 44.6% of the resident population. However, this does not reflect the national picture, with non-white ethnic minorities comprising less than 6% of the total UK population*.

Half-Caste

is generally avoided. It ignores the person's ethnic and national identity and implies that they are inadequate or incomplete. It also has negative associations with the caste system in India.

Immigrant

describes someone who has left their own country and travelled to another in order to live and work. In some countries like America and Australia, the population is made up almost entirely of former immigrants. The original inhabitants (in this case, the Native Americans and Aborigines respectively) were almost wiped out, reduced by genocide, war, disease and poverty to a national minority.

In Britain the term IMMIGRANT is generally avoided, particularly when referring to the younger generation. Nearly half of all black people in this country were born here – and well over half of those who came to Britain as immigrants have now been here for in excess of 20 years. When used in the media, the term rarely includes white immigrants (from Australia or South Africa, for example). This was most obvious when Margaret Thatcher made her famous comment in the mid-eighties voicing her fears that immigrants might 'swamp' British culture.

> * These figures are based on the 1991 National Census, and are generally thought to be an underestimation. More precise data about ethnic minorities can be obtained from your local authority or from your Race Equality or Community Relations Council.

Migrant

refers to people who have travelled from one country to another, typically for work or for economic motives. Migrants often become first generation immigrants when their plans to return home fall through, or when marriage, children and other ties require them to settle down in their host country on a more permanent basis.

Mixed Parentage

is the term usually preferred by people whose parents come from more than one racial, national or ethnic group. They may also refer to their mixed or 'DUAL HERITAGE' or identify themselves by referring to their parents' nationality (e.g. Anglo-Nigerian, half Indian-half Scottish etc). Many people of mixed heritage also choose to identify themselves as 'black' arguing that having one white parent makes little difference in a society where racism is so entrenched. However, this view is contested by some white mothers in America and Britain, who argue that it denies their children's white heritage to call them 'black'.

People of Colour

is the umbrella term commonly used in the United States to refer to descendants of (non-white) immigrant and slave communities such as African Americans, Puerto Ricans and Koreans but the term hasn't caught on here in Britain.

Refugee and Asylum-seeker

the term REFUGEE is defined under Article 1 of the 1951 UN Convention as a person who 'owing to well-founded fear of being persecuted for reasons of 'race', religion, nationality, membership of a particular social group or political opinion, is outside the country of his (sic) nationality and is unable or, owing to such fear, is unwilling to avail himself of the protection of that country; or who, not having a nationality and being outside the country of his habitual residence as a result of such events, is unable or, owing to such fear, is unwilling to return to it'.

The term ASYLUM-SEEKER describes people who have applied for political asylum either before, after or on entering the country, and are awaiting official leave to remain here. Recent changes in the law have meant that this is now the status of the vast majority of people who seek refuge or asylum in Britain. Because of the needy, dependent connotations of the term 'asylum seeker' and its negative associations in the media, 'NEW ARRIVALS' is the more neutral term increasingly preferred by those who provide services to this group.

Visible Minority

is used increasingly as an alternative to Ethnic Minority. Some people see it as is a less ambiguous way of identifying non-white groups. However, both terms are problematic and as society becomes increasingly diverse, the term 'minority' may also have to be reviewed.

WORDS THAT DESCRIBE WHAT WE DO AND HOW WE VIEW THINGS

Antiracism

describes the conscious effort people make to challenge and combat racism in all its behavioural and institutional forms.

Colourism

is a term coined by Alice Walker, an African-American writer, to refer to the negative attitudes within black communities towards a person's skin tone. Traditionally, lighter-skinned people were afforded more privileges in Africa and the Caribbean, causing some black parents to favour their lighter-skinned children.

Culture

refers to the shared rituals, symbols and practices that give a group or individual their sense of who they are and help them make sense of the world they live in. Expressed through music, language, food, dress, art etc., culture is a dynamic (i.e. constantly changing) concept that may include – but is not necessarily the same as – someone's personal beliefs or moral values. So not all skinheads are racists; not all people with dreadlocks are Rastafarians (etc).

Direct Discrimination

involves treating one person less favourably than others on the grounds of their 'race', colour, nationality (including citizenship) or religion, or because of their ethnic or national origins. It is outlawed under Article 14 of the European Convention for the Protection of Human Rights and Fundamental Rights and Freedoms, to which all European member states including the UK are signatories. Here in Britain, the Race Relations Act makes both direct and indirect discrimination on the grounds of 'race', colour or national origin illegal.

Ethnocentricity

involves seeing the world from perspective of a particular ethnic group, often with the assumption that the values, beliefs and achievements of that group are superior to those of other ethnic groups. All groups have the ability to be ethnocentric. Black people descended from Africa, for instance, have sometimes found it necessary to adopt an AFROCENTRIC approach to the study of history, art, science and literature, promoting black people's achievements in order to make up for the fact that historically they have tended to be invisible.

Eurocentricity

EUROCENTRIC assumptions are still at the root of much of what we learn in school. They stem from the view that European (Western) civilisation is superior and should therefore be regarded as a reference point for all others.

Indirect Discrimination

involves applying a rule, condition or requirement or behaving in way that results in less favourable conditions or treatment for a particular individual or group. This could involve enforcing a certain dress code or a school timetable that does not take account of someone's religious obligations. The Race Relations Act makes indirect discrimination on the grounds of 'race' illegal unless there is an 'objective justification' – i.e. unless it can be justified on other grounds

Institutional Racism

refers to those practices, policies and procedures in an organisation or institution (e.g. a school or a hospital) that support or encourage direct or indirect racial discrimination or give rise to racial disadvantage. Originating in America with the rise of the Black Power movement, the Macpherson report has defined it as: 'The collective failure of an organisation to provide an appropriate and professional service to people because of their colour, culture or ethnic origin. It can been seen or detected in processes, attitudes and behaviour which amount to discrimination through unwitting prejudice, ignorance, thoughtlessness or racial stereotyping'. While institutional racism may well be unconscious or unwitting, as Macpherson suggests, it can also be calculated and deliberate.

Multiculturalism

describes a situation where there are many different cultures in a society, and when the available services and facilities (for example, health, education, the arts etc.) recognise this fact in a positive way. The term describes both an approach (e.g. multicultural education) and a vision (e.g. multicultural society).

Nationalism

describes the sentiment felt by a group of people who share a distinct sense of cultural or historical identity or believe they have a common destiny because they are citizens of a particular country, nation or continent. Extreme nationalism has resulted in acts of genocide or 'ethnic cleansing', justified by the dominant group's belief in their 'natural' or god-given superiority.

North/ South

These terms have been in popular use since the early eighties, to contrast poorer countries of the South with the richer, industrialised countries in the North (or 'the West'). However, it is worth remembering that there are poor countries in the Northern hemisphere, just as there are some rich countries in the South.

Prejudice

occurs when someone pre-judges a particular group or individual based on their own stereotypical assumptions or ignorance

Positive Action

describes the special measures that can be taken to help people who are disadvantaged because of prejudice, stereotyping or discrimination (for example in employment or schooling). In the USA it is referred to as AFFIRMATIVE ACTION. It usually refers to a practical attempt to encourage people to take full and equal advantage of opportunities in jobs, education, training or other areas. Positive Action is not the same as Positive (or 'Reverse') Discrimination which involves giving preferential treatment to a particular individual or group. This remains illegal in the UK.

'Race'

is a term used less and less these days because it refers to a concept that few people believe in anymore. The idea that people belong to different 'races' was developed in the 18th and 19th centuries in an attempt to explain the many differences between people. Scientists and philosophers of the day divided humankind into three racial groups based entirely on superficial differences in skin-colour, hair texture, eye shape etc. Ever since then, this pseudo-scientific 'evidence' has been used to reinforce the belief that people's physical, intellectual and behavioural differences are hereditary. Genetic research has shown that underneath the 'paintwork', human beings are essentially the same, meaning that people's skin colour is of little more relevance than the colour of their eyes or hair.

Racial Harassment

involves acts of verbal or physical abuse and other forms of threatening behaviour towards people of another racial or ethnic group. It is likely to be persistent and is usually (though not always) intentional. It includes persistent name-calling, bullying, ridicule, the use of graffiti or abusive language and acts of racially-motivated violence.

Racism

describes a complex set of attitudes and behaviour towards people from another racial or ethnic group, most commonly based on...

- the belief that differences in physical/cultural characteristics (such as skin colour, language, dress, religious practices, etc.) correspond directly to differences in personality, intelligence or ability, leading to assumptions about racial superiority and inferiority

- the social or economic power of members of one racial or ethnic group to promote, enforce or 'act out' such attitudes

Racist views and attitudes usually lead to discriminatory behaviour and practices that, in turn, contribute to inequality and social exclusion.

Right-wing Extremism

is based on notions of superior racial or national identity and a group's shared belief in its exclusive cultural, historical or national identity (see nationalism). Extreme right-wing (sometimes referred to as 'fascist' or 'far right') activity is widespread in Britain and mainland Europe, and has been responsible for countless acts of racially-motivated violence, including genocide, 'ethnic cleansing', arson and murder. There are extreme right-wing parties in every country in Europe, some even represented in parliament. The British National Party (BNP) won a seat in local elections in the Isle of Dogs, East London, as recently as 1992*.

Stereotyping

involves labelling or categorising particular groups of people, usually in a negative way, according to pre-conceived ideas or broad generalisations about them – and then assuming that all members of that group will think and behave identically.

Third World

refers to under-industrialised countries outside Europe and America. Some people prefer to say 'the two-thirds world', the developing world or 'the South', arguing that terms like 'third world' or 'under-developed' are patronising and eurocentric.

Xenophobia

describes extreme feelings of fear or hostility towards outsiders. It can be expressed through a person's subconscious attitudes or their views and actions in response to individuals or groups from a different national, ethnic, religious or cultural background.

94

* This was subsequently reversed, although support for the BNP and other neo-Nazi groups in Britain like Blood and Honour and Combat 18 remains widespread in some areas where white working class youth are still actively recruited.

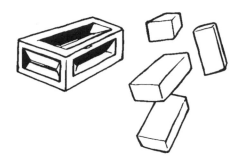

BOOKS AND RESOURCES

This list is by no means exhaustive. However, it will serve as a starting point for people wishing to develop their knowledge base in the different areas covered in this *Toolkit*. To obtain an up-to-date list of what else is available, bookshops that specialise in 'black' books are probably your best starting point. Most will have catalogue of their titles. The Working Group Against Racism in Children's Books can supply you with a list of bookshops in different cities that you could visit.

If you have access to the Internet, you could also keep an eye on the website pages of major publishers like PLUTO PRESS, ROUTLEDGE, RUNNYMEDE TRUST, OPEN UNIVERSITY PRESS, SAGE, TRENTHAM BOOKS and others that publish in books this area. You may also want to check the websites of Organisations and Universities with research departments that specialise in Racial Discrimination and Diversity – for example, the **Institute of Race Relations**, which has been at the forefront of research in this area for many years; or the **University of Warwick's Centre for Research in Ethnic Relations,** which produces regular analyses of census data (invaluable for benchmarking purposes) and some useful research papers (again, see Useful Addresses).

Antiracism and Multiculturalism in Schools

There is a growing number of books and journals that explore the development of anti-racism and multiculturalism in UK schools. If you would like more insight into the issues covered in the introduction, or the policies and practices that have informed anti-racist/multicultural initiatives over the past thirty years, start by reading one or more of the following, and exploring their Bibliographies for other titles that would interest you:

❑ *Inclusive Schools, Inclusive society* Robin Richardson for Race on the Agenda (Trentham Books, 1999)
This is an impressive and very accessible resource that sets out the practical measures schools can adopt in order to become more inclusive. Using a wealth of source materials, each chapter focuses on the complex issues that surround schools' handling of racism, culture and identity. The introduction includes some useful statistical data on the achievement rates of black and other ethnic minority children at Key Stage 2 and GCSE which could be helpful for benchmarking purposes.

❑ *Racism and Antiracism in Real Schools* by David Gillborn (Open University Press 1995)
This book will give you a firm grasp of how antiracist policies and practices have developed over the past three decades as well as an appreciation of the key issues facing teachers, students, managers and policy-makers in the millennium. It includes a comprehensive bibliography.

❑ *Education Towards Race Equality* by Gillian Klein (Cassell, 1993)
Gives a clear, historical account of the way politicians and policy-makers have responded to the different issues and concerns in this area, and some practical guidance on school management, classroom organisation and curriculum development.

More Than Skin Deep: Developing antiracist multicultural education in schools by Ian Massey (Hodder and Stoughton, 1991)
Contains a useful account of the different controversies that have informed antiracist debates in schools over the years, and some useful references for schools in 'all-white' areas.

Still No Problem Here by Chris Gaine (Trentham Books, 1995)
Provides a helpful summary of some of the main theoretical issues and debates, along with some practical strategies for schools in all-white catchment areas

MCT Multicultural Teaching (Trentham Books)
This is a quarterly journal that addresses all aspects of teaching and learning in a multicultural society. A vital resource if you want to keep up to date with the latest debates and issues, books and resources, conferences and courses etc. that address this subject

Meeting Legal Requirements

Advice is available from the Commission for Racial Equality (CRE) or your local Race Equality Council on measures to prevent racial harassment and racial discrimination in schools. If in doubt, it may also be advisable to refer to the CRE's published codes of practice for eliminating racism in schools and employment, since these codes have statutory force and failure to follow their recommendations can be cited as evidence in a case of alleged racial discrimination. These and other CRE publications can be ordered by telephoning (0207 828 7022

- ❑ **Code of Practice for the Elimination of Racial Discrimination in Education**
- ❑ **Code of Practice for the Elimination of Racial Discrimination in Employment**
- ❑ **Lessons of the Law: A Casebook of Racial Discrimination in Education**

Policy Development

If you are developing or revising your policy or looking for examples of good practice in this area, any of the following publications would be a good place to start:

- ❑ *Equal Opportunities: A Quick Guide* **by G.Hughes and W.Smith (Daniels, 1995)**
  A handy little book aimed at teachers in schools who want practical guidance on designing, formulating, writing and implementing your EO policy.

- ❑ *Equality in Action: Introducing EO in Voluntary Organisations* **by Mee-Yang Cheung-Judge and Alix Henley (NCVO, 1994)**
  Aimed at the voluntary sector, this book is just as relevant to schools and other organisations. It provides a step-by-step approach to policy development as well as practical exercises that can be used to achieve positive and lasting institutional change.

- ❑ *Racism and Education: Structures and Strategies* **by Dawn Gill, Barbara Major and Maud Blair (Open University Press, 1992)**
  A collection of essays about policy-making at different levels, with descriptions of some of the practical projects schools have initiated in this area.

- ❑ *Race and Gender: EO policies in Education*, **Open University Press, (1995)**

Exclusions and Achievement

These are key issues for all schools to address. For a better understanding of the arguments, statistical evidence and available strategies, including the need to work in partnership with parents, try any of the following:

- ❑ *Recent Research on the Achievements of Minority Ethnic Pupils* **by David Gillborn and Caroline Gipps (OFSTED, 1996)**
  A very useful investigative report on the attainment of Bangladeshi, Black Caribbean, Pakistani and Traveller children in schools that summaries the implications for schools and LEAs and describes a number of school-based initiatives to raise achievement.

- ❑ *Raising the Attainment of Minority Ethnic Pupils: School and LEA Responses* **(OFSTED, 1999)**

- ❑ *Making the Difference: teaching and learning stretegies in successful multi-ethnic schools* **by Maud Blair, Jill Bourne et al, (DfEE) 1998)**
  Theory, case studies and practice that enables cultural-minority students to succeed.

- ❑ *Improving Practice: A whole-school approach to raising the achievement of African Caribbean youth* **by Debbie Weekes and Cecile Wright (Runnymede Trust, 1998)**

- ❑ *Exclusion from Secondary Schools* **(OFSTED, 1995/96)**

- ❑ *Exclusions: A discussion document* **(HMSO, 1992)**
  Also vital reading, these two reports will help you explore the issues surrounding school exclusions and consider some of the implications for schools wishing to reduce their exclusion rates

- ❑ *Exclusion from School and Racial Equality* **by Audrey Osler (CRE, 1997)**

- *Race, Class and Gender in Exclusion from School* by Cecile Wright *et al.* (Falmer Press, 1999)
- *Outcast England: How Schools Exclude Black Children* (Institute of Race Relations, 1994)

- *Young, Gifted and Black, Student Teacher Relations in the Schooling of Black Youth* by M. Mac an Ghaill, Open University Press, 1988

- *Working with Parents: a whole-school approach* by J. Bastiani (Routledge, 1989)

- *Involving Parents* by Alastair Macbeth (Heinemann, 1989)

Racial Discrimination

When tackling racism as a policy or curriculum issue, particularly if the subject is new to you, it is wise to do some reading and thinking about racial discrimination in advance. Much research has been done on this subject, and there are some excellent books and teaching resources available.

- *Racism and Discrimination in Britain Today: A Select Bibliography* (Runnymede Trust latest edition)
  Use this bibliography for an up-to-date list of publications that will help you to explore specific aspects of racism and discrimination in Britain.

- *Dictionary of Race and Ethnic Relations*, E.Ellis Cashmore (Routledge latest edition)
  A quick route to understanding the many terms and events that have defined race and ethnic relations in Britain. Cross-referenced, it also includes some useful suggestions for further reading,

- *Race in Britain Today* by Richard Skillington (Sage, 1996)
  Drawing on both official data and alternative research, this book will give you a wealth of statistical information as well as a summary of current debates and controversies about the effectiveness of antiracist policies in education, employment, the criminal justice system and other areas. Particularly useful if you are looking for statistical evidence or want some raw data for students to analyse.

- *Racism in Children's Lives: a study of mainly-white schools* by Barry Troyna and Richard Hatcher (Routledge, 1992)
  Looks at how racism and racist views influence the lives and attitudes of children in mainly white schools

- *Islamophobia: a challenge for us all* (Runnymede Trust, 1997)

- *Learning in Terror* (CRE, 1987)
  Case study accounts of the racial harassment and bullying experienced by children in and on the way to school.

- *Murder in the Playground: The Burnage Report* by Ian Macdonald *et al* (Longsight Press, 1989)
  This report into the inquiry into the murder of Ahmed Ullah highlights many important issues in antiracist and multicultural education, as well as giving some useful pointers for managers and headteachers

Challenging Racism

For ideas and activities for challenging racism, try any of the following:

- *Racetracks: a resource pack for tackling racism with youth people*, Stella Dadzie (LB of Greenwich, 1993)
  A practical guide aimed at youth workers that contains a wealth of practical ideas and activities for challenging racism in all-white or ethnically-mixed contexts, as well as some useful resource sheets addressing historical and contemporary issues.

- *Spanner in the Works: Education for racial equality and social justice in white schools* by Clare Brown *et al* (Trentham Books, 1990)
  Cross-curricular approaches to teaching children about racism and exploring their own and others' feelings

- *When Hate Comes to Town: community responses to racism and fascism* (Searchlight, 1995)
  A comprehensive resource pack that focuses on the activities and philosophies of far-right organisations and suggests community-based strategies for combating them – and the ideas they promote

- *Challenging Racism, Valuing Difference – a facilitator's guide* (Tower Hamlets Learning Design Centre, 1994)

❑   *Learning About Racism: an introduction for use in schools* (Runnymede Trust, 1988)

❑   *Tackling Racism: a secondary school course* (LB Newham/ Education Dept)

❑   *Teaching Against Prejudice and Stereotyping: a practical handbook for 15-19 year olds* (Oxford Polytechnic Development Education Unit, 1986)

History

A basic understanding of the history of black (African-Caribbean, Asian and other ethnic minority) people and their motives for coming to Britain is essential if you are to address the issues raised in this *Toolkit* with confidence. There are numerous books and learning resources on the subject, and it is worth obtaining an up-to-date list from your librarian. Their list will probably include some of the following:

❑   *Staying Power: the History of Black People in Britain* by Peter Fryer (Pluto Press, 1985)
A comprehensive and very readable study that begins with the Romans, takes you through slavery, colonialism and migration to Britain, and ends with the urban disturbances of the early 1980s.

❑   *Black People in the British empire: An Introduction* by Peter Fryer (Pluto Press, 1988)
This is a shorter version of *Staying Power* and focuses on Britain's colonial relationship with India, Africa and other parts of the world. Useful if you want an insight into the maxim 'we are here because you were there'...

❑   *Homebeats: Struggles for Racial Justice* (Institute of Race Relations,1998)
For those with access to a CD-rom, this is an excellent way of developing your knowledge and historical awareness. Described as 'a multi-media journey through time from the Caribbean, Asian and Africa to the making of modern Britain', it allows you to access Memories, People, Places, Visions and Images from the main menu and offers hundreds of pathways through the material, depending on your interests.

❑   *How Racism Came to Britain* (Institute of Race Relations, 1985)
This was the last of a series specifically aimed at young people of secondary school age. Presented in a humorous, cartoon format, this is still available and is still relevant today.

❑   *Nothing But the Same Old Story: the Roots of Anti-Irish Racism* by Liz Curtis *et al.* (Information on Ireland, 1992)
Gives an overview of the historical relationship between Britain and Ireland, and explains why and how the Irish have been depicted over the centuries.

❑   *Reclaiming Our Pasts* by Hilary Claire (Trentham, 1996)
All the information needed to make the KS1 and 2 programmes of study for History truly inclusive.

❑   *From Prejudice to Genocide: Learning about the Holocaust* by Carrie Supple (Trentham Books, 1993, new edition 1999)
Describes the persecution of Travellers and Jews before and during the Nazi era and examines 'the final solution' through the eyes of survivors as well as contemporary commentary.

❑   *The Heart of the Race* by B.Bryan, S.Dadzie, S.Scafe (Virago, 1985)
Uses interviews with black women to describe the experiences of African-Caribbean women and their communities – both historically and in the years since the war. Useful if you are looking for first person accounts of racism or examples of how racism can affect women's lives.

Culture and Identity

Whether your aim is to explore these issues in the classroom or to raise your own awareness, the following books will provide you with some useful and challenging insights:

❑ *The Light in Their Eyes: Creating multicultural learning communities* (Teachers College Press and Trentham Books, 1999)
Theory case studies and practice that enables cultural-minority students to succeed

❑ *Critical Multiculturalism: Rethinking multicultural and antiracist education* ed. Stephen May (Open University Press, 1999)

❑ *Black Masculinities and Schooling: How Black boys survive modern schooling* by Tony Sewell (Trentham Books, 1997)

❑ *Children of Islam: a teacher's guide to meeting the needs of Muslim pupils* by Marie Parker-Jenkins (Trentham Books, 1995)

❑ *Educating Somali Children in Britain* by Mohamed Kahin (Trentham Books, 1997)

❑ *Hindu Children in Britain* by Robert and Nesbitt Jackson (Trentham Books, 1993)

❑ *The Changing Face of Britain: A guide to the customs, traditions and lifestyles of Britain's Minority Ethnic communities* (West Midlands Police, 1993)
Available by telephoning West Midlands Police Community Service Department on 0121 626 5000 ext. 2321)

Curriculum

If you are involved in curriculum planning activities, the following texts will give you an insight into some of the debates and available strategies in this area, as well as ideas for different subject areas:

❑ *Equality Assurance in Schools: Quality, Identity, Society – A Handbook for action planning and school effectiveness* (Runnymede Trust with Trentham Books, 1993)
This is vital reading for anyone wanting to ensure that all subject areas address race equality, identity, cultural diversity, citizenship and entitlement issues while meeting the requirements of the National Curriculum. It provides good practice indicators for all subject areas, with examples of activities to support them. The bibliography provides a wealth of sources for teachers of Art, English, Geography, History, Maths, Music, PE, Religious Education, Science and Technology. It also contains general guidance on Equality Assurance, the requirements of the National Curriculum and what inspectors look for.

❑ *The Multicultural Dimension of the National Curriculum* edited by Anna King and Michael Reiss (Falmer, 1993)

❑ *International Dimensions of the National Curriculum* by Rex Andrews (Trentham Books, 1994)

❑ **Working Group Against Racism in Children's Resources** produces excellent checklists for vetting children's books and teaching resources, as well as keeping subscribers informed about novels and other titles that can be ordered for the library

Multi-Ethnic Britain

Few books do justice to the diversity of multi-ethnic Britain – your best resource is probably the children you teach and their respective communities. Nevertheless, the following texts will give you some insights into multi-ethnic Britain and the lives and experiences of different ethnic minority groups.

❑ *Roots of the Future: Ethnic Diversity in the Making of Britain* (CRE, 1997)
This is a CRE publication that looks at immigration and the contribution of ethnic minorities in Britain. Copies are available by telephoning Central Books on 0181 986 5488.

❑ **Refugees in Today's Europe: a Video Action Pack (International Broadcasting Trust, 1991)**
The pack includes a video, teachers' notes and activity sheets that focus on the experiences of refugees and asylum seekers. *The REFUGEE COUNCIL* (Address on p.101) will supply a free resource list on request on *Teaching and Learning about Refugees*

❑ ***In the Midst of the Whirlwind: A manual for helping refugee children*** by Naomi Richman (Trentham Books, 1998)
Written for teachers, social and health workers, this book addresses the experiences of refugee children and their families and sets out an agenda for agencies wishing to address their needs

❑ ***A Visible Presence – Black People Living and Working in Britain Today***
An annotated booklist for Young Adults, Teachers, Librarians and Community Workers (National Book League) that will give you an overview of what else is available.

Videos

Television documentaries and films can be an excellent way of introducing racism and exploring its effects on individuals and society. Even programmes made over a decade ago can still have a lot to offer. As well as the BBC and Channel 4, most major broadcasting companies have education departments offering videos of programmes that have been broadcast on TV either for sale or hire. These are often accompanied by excellent back-up notes for teachers and it is worth keeping an eye on their websites for information on what is available. Up-to-date catalogues of the many films and videos you could use to support the activities listed in Part 2 of this Toolkit are available from the following sources:

❑ Academy Television, 104 Kirkstall Rd, Lees LS3 1JS 01523 461528

❑ Albany Videos, Battersea Studios, TV Centre, Thackeray Rd, London SW8 0207 498 6811

❑ BBC Enterprises, Woodlands, 80 Wood Lane, Ealing, London W12 OTT 0208 749 0538

❑ British Film and Video Library, British Film Institute, 21 Stephen Street, London W1P 1PL 0207 255 1444

❑ Concorde Video and Film Council, 201 Felixtowe Rd, Ipswich 1P3 9BJ 01473 76012

❑ International Broadcasting Trust, Education Officer, IBT, 2 Ferdinand Place, London NW1 8EE 0207 482 2847

❑ MOSAIC, BBC Education, Room 404, Villiers House, Ealing, London W5 2P

❑ Swingbridge Video, Norden House, 41 Stomwell Street, Newcastle upon Tyne, NE1 4YB. 091 232 3762

Campaign against Racism and Fascism
BM Box 8784
London WC1XN 3XX
Produces a regular newsletter that will keep you up to date on all aspects of racism and fascism in the UK.

Centre for Multicultural Education
Institute of Education (University of London)
20 Bedford Way
London WC1H OAL

Centre for Research in Ethnic Relations
University of Warwick
Coventry CV4 7AL
01203 524324
Produces regular analyses of census data (invaluable for benchmarking purposes) as well as publishing some useful research papers.

Commission for Racial Equality
Elliot House
10-12 Allington Street
London SW1E 5EH
0207 828 7022

Department for Education and Employment (DfEE)
DfEE publications
PO Box 5050
Nottingham NG15 ODJ
0845 602 2260
For copies of DfEE good practice guides and study reports.

The Festival Shop
50 Poplar Rd
Birmingham B14 7AG
0121 444 0444
Order their catalogue – they have some wonderful posters for sale, as well as maps, books about different cultures and the Festival Year Calendar which gives information about all the main religions in Britain and gives dates and details about major festivals.

Institute of Race Relations
2-4 Leeke Street, London WC1X 9HS
0207 837 0041
The IRR produced the CD-rom HOMEBEATS, has a comprehensive research library and can also offer helpful advice about books and other resources you might wish to access. They produce *RACE and CLASS* quarterly, published by Sage.

Minority Rights Group
379 Brixton Rd
London SW9 7DE
0207 978 9498
MRG produces up-to-date reports about many different ethnic minority groups, including Kurds, Eritreans, Sri Lankans, Cypriots and others

New Beacon Books
76 Stroud Green Road
London N4
020 7272 4889
Specialists in African and African-Caribbean books, including a large selection of books for children and young people.

Race On The Agenda
356 Holloway Rd
London N7 6PA
0207 700 8135
ROTA provides a policy development, information and research service for London's Black and Minority Ethnic voluntary sector and produced *Inclusive Schools, Inclusive Society*

Reading and Language Information Centre
University of Reading
Bulmershe Court, Early
Reading RG6 1HY
0118 931 8820
Maintains a database of resources for use in schools and will supply an up-to-date list on request.

Refugee Council
3-9 Bondway
London SW8 1SJ
0207 582 6922
The Refugee Council can supply a free resource list for Teaching and Learning about Refugees, as well as a list of refugee organisations. They can also put you in touch with potential speakers

Runnymede Trust
133 Aldersgate Street
London EC1A 4JA
0207 375 1496
The Runnymede Trust is an education charity that researches race equality issues and provides publications, information and advice on race-related issues. Get on their mailing list or check their website for an up-to-date list.

Soma Books
38 Kennington Lane
London SE11
0207 735 2101
Specialises in books and artifacts from India and Africa for children and adults.

The Stationery Office
Holborn Bookshop
49 High Holborn
London WC1X
0207 873 0011 (general enquiries) or 0207 873 9090 (telephone orders)

Working Group Against Racism in Children's Resources
46 Wandsworth Rd
London SW8 3LX
0207 627 4594
Produces excellent checklists for vetting children's books and teaching resources, as well as keeping subscribers informed of new books that can be ordered for the library

Stella Dadzie *is of Anglo-Ghanaian parentage. She began her career as a teacher and has many years' experience of working in education, in secondary schools, colleges, with young offenders and with adult learners. She is currently a training consultant, specialising in Race and other equality issues. Her publications include:*

- THE HEART OF THE RACE: Black Women's Lives in Britain by B.Bryan, S.Dadzie and S.Scafe (Virago, 1985)
- EDUCATIONAL GUIDANCE WITH BLACK COMMUNITIES: A Checklist of Good Practice (NIACE, 1990)
- ESSENTIAL SKILLS FOR RACE EQUALITY TRAINERS (NIACE, 1992)
- OLDER and WISER: A Study of Educational Provision for Black and Ethnic Minority Elders (NIACE, 1992)
- WORKING WITH BLACK ADULT LEARNERS: a Practical Guide (NIACE, 1993)
- RACETRACKS: A Resource Pack for Tackling Racism with Young People (LB Greenwich, 1993)
- BLOOD, SWEAT and TEARS: An Account of the Bede AntiRacist Detached Youth Work Project (National Youth Agency, July 1997)
- ADULT EDUCATION IN MULTI-ETHNIC EUROPE: A Handbook for Organisational Change (European Commission/ IIZ-DVV, Bonn) 1998
- EQUALITY ASSURANCE: Self Assessment for Equal Opportunities in Further Education (FEDA, 1998)
- AUDITING FOR EQUALITY: Auditing Council Performance against REMQ (CRE, 1999)
- EQUALITY ASSURANCE: Self-Assessment for Equal Opportunities in Training (DfEE/TEC National Council, 1999).
- VISUAL REALITIES: An AntiRacism Guide for Teachers and Youth Workers (Camden Race Equality Council, 1999) – companion to the video
- MAKING A DIFFERENCE: A Resource for People who want to become more Active Citizens (NIACE, 1999)